YORK

General Edito
of Stirling) & 1
University of E

Susan Hill

I'M THE KING
OF THE CASTLE

Notes by Hana Sambrook

MA PH D (EDINBURGH)

LONGMAN
YORK PRESS

YORK PRESS
Immeuble Esseily, Place Riad Solh, Beirut.

LONGMAN GROUP UK LIMITED
Longman House, Burnt Mill, Harlow,
Essex CM20 2JE, England
Associated companies, branches and representatives
throughout the world

First published in 1992

ISBN 0-582-09642-1

Phototypeset by Gem Graphics, Trenance, Mawgan Porth, Cornwall
Printed in Hong Kong
WC/01

Contents

Part 1

Introduction

The life of Susan Hill

Susan Elizabeth Hill was born on 5 February 1942 at Scarborough in Yorkshire, and was educated at the grammar school there and in Coventry, West Midlands. An only child, she was a voracious reader, and her love of reading remained with her: she went on to study English literature at King's College, London, where she graduated BA Honours in English in 1963.

Her first book, *The Enclosure*, came out in 1961, followed in 1963 by *Do Me a Favour*. Then came *Gentleman and Ladies* and *A Change for the Better*, both published in 1969, *I'm the King of the Castle*, 1970 (awarded the Somerset Maugham Prize), *The Albatross and Other Stories*, 1971 (winner of the John Llewelyn Rhys Memorial Prize). *Strange Meeting* was also published in 1971, followed in 1972 by *The Bird of Night* (winner of the Whitbread Award). Another book of short stories appeared in 1973 under the title *A Bit of Singing and Dancing*, and then came *In the Springtime of the Year* in 1974. After a considerable gap her latest novel, *Air and Angels*, was published in 1991.

As well as a formidable number of works of fiction (all the more formidable if we consider the novelist's age during these years of prodigious creativity), she published *The Cold Country and Other Plays for Radio* in 1975, *The Magic Apple Tree* (a record of her life in an Oxfordshire village) in 1982, a ghost story, *The Woman in Black*, in 1983 (adapted for the stage in 1989), *Through the Kitchen Window* (another record of village life) in 1984. In 1986 she published *Through the Garden Gate* and in 1987 *The Lighting of the Lamps* and *Lanterns across the Snow* (a child's memories of Christmas in Wessex during the last century). Two works followed to testify to her love of the English countryside: *Shakespeare Country* (1987) and *The Spirit of the Cotswolds* (1988). In 1989 she published an autobiographical work, *Family*.

She has also written several books for children, edited two books of ghost stories, and a selection of short stories (*The Distracted Preacher and Other Tales*) by Thomas Hardy with whom she shares her love of the country as well as her dark vision of the human predicament.

During the years 1977–86 she wrote the literary column for the *Daily Telegraph*, and from 1986 to 1987 she was presenter of 'Bookshelf' on BBC Radio 4. Her love of English literature is strikingly evident in all her activities: she writes books, she edits, reviews and discusses books, she shares her passion for books with her readers and listeners.

She is married to the Shakespeare scholar Stanley Wells, and has two daughters. Another child, a girl, died in infancy.

Since her marriage in 1975 until quite recently she has written little fiction, the reason being, as she said in a radio interview, that she has been 'too happy' to write novels. This might seem a strange reason to give until we consider the nature of her novels. They deal overwhelmingly with misfits, with people who have been bereaved, disappointed and embittered, with victimised children, with pain and death. The countryside in which she delights in private life becomes in her novels a mirror reflecting human suffering – the predatory crow, the thrush savaging a snail, both are symbols of the destructive pain people inflict on one another.

Children in fiction

I'm the King of the Castle is a book about children; nothing unusual about that, you might say. There are a great many novels featuring children, of course. Any book which begins with the hero's or heroine's childhood will fall into this category. Think for instance of Charles Dickens's *David Copperfield* (1850) and his *Great Expectations* (1861), think of Charlotte Brontë's *Jane Eyre* (1847), of James Joyce's *A Portrait of the Artist as a Young Man* (1916), all of which portray childhood, its joys and, especially, its miseries, with great force. In these novels the scenes from childhood serve to show that the child is indeed the father of the man, and help the reader to understand the adult hero's or heroine's character in the light of experiences undergone in childhood. (Charles Dickens's intuitive understanding of children is unsurpassed, but always it is the grown man looking back and inviting the reader to share and understand the past – and to pity the child.)

Then there are novels which, though intended for adults, include children among their main characters, sometimes placing them at the very centre of the novel: Dickens's *Oliver Twist* (1838), Henry James's ghost tale *The Turn of the Screw* (1898) and his *What Maisie Knew* (1897), Richard Hughes's *A High Wind in Jamaica* (1929), L. P. Hartley's *Eustace and Hilda* trilogy (1944–7), Harper Lee's *To Kill a Mockingbird* (1960). In these novels the child plays a significant part in the plot, as distinct from characterisation. Indeed the child may become the main agent of the plot, sometimes unwittingly, like the boy Leo in L. P. Hartley's *The Go-Between* (1953) whose role in the love affair between an upper-class girl and her farmer lover ultimately leads to tragedy, or the little girl Scout in Harper Lee's *To Kill a Mockingbird* who brings about the death of the man who is trying to murder her. Maisie in Henry James's *What Maisie Knew* is an innocent among corrupt adults, emphasising their tainted nature through her own guileless ignorance. The children in James's *The Turn of the Screw* are not innocent, having been corrupted by the evil Quint, but they are still only tools, and their part in the plot is a passive one. The centre of the novelist's interest here is their young governess, and we see the two corrupted children entirely through her eyes, while observing the effect of her discoveries about them upon her.

By contrast, in Richard Hughes's *A High Wind in Jamaica*, Emily, who in the course of the novel moves from childhood to a hypocritical girlhood, is the direct and knowing agent of the death on the scaffold of the pirate captain and his men. She no longer is the innocent bystander, the adults' tool, far from it; she acts to save herself by accusing others. Yet she is still a child in an adult world.

What distinguishes Susan Hill's novel is that here the adults become the bystanders while the drama is acted out between the two boys. Here it is a child who is evil: Edmund torments Charles knowingly and delights in doing so. His reaction on seeing Charles's dead body is one of triumph: 'I did that, *it was because of me.*' In her Afterword the novelist herself defines this quality in Edmund's nature as evil which possesses him, but unless we take her words literally he is not an instrument of another, supernatural force; he acts as he does of his own free will and for his own pleasure: he *is* evil.

Susan Hill's novel has been compared to William Golding's book *Lord of the Flies* (1954), and certainly both novels possess qualities which set them apart from other works of fiction featuring children. Both are about children but were not written for children. They convey with a terrible clarity the pain that children are capable of inflicting on one another, and they both deal with evil in a child. While Hill seems a little reluctant to accept at last that Edmund Hooper is evil, Golding has no difficulty in identifying evil as such, taking a moralistic stance and seeing man as born cruel and evil and reverting to this state of original sin once the restraints of civilisation cease to operate. Working within the framework of Christian theology, however, he is ready to acknowledge the existence not only of evil, but of goodness and sacrifice as well.

We might see these two novels as representing a new development in the role given to children in fiction. The nineteenth-century novel, reflecting the general view of the place of children in society, gives children a role which, while contributing to the characterisation of the adult heroes and heroines, remains subservient. They are idealised, sentimentalised, and ultimately marginalised.

A more recent development, belonging to the twentieth century, finds the child playing an important, often crucial part in the plot. Sometimes a knowing agent, sometimes an innocent tool, the child is still surrounded and overshadowed by adults, and is seen as intrinsically different, innocent or ignorant, and helpless.

In Susan Hill's *I'm the King of the Castle*, however, as in William Golding's novel, we observe a change: the child may be helpless because of material, external limitations on his freedom of behaviour, but in his own world he is no different from the adult. He may be kind or cruel because that is his nature, not because he is a child. In Golding's novel particularly, the nineteenth-century tradition of depicting children as innocent victims comes to an abrupt end, with a return to the theological doctrines of earlier centuries which saw man as born sinful and remaining so even in his childhood.

In contrast Susan Hill is not concerned with the large issues of good and evil; her concern is with two boys, one wicked, the other a victim whose brief life ends in pain. Where for Golding evil is universal, erupting when civilisation collapses, for Hill evil is there in one child, like a hideous disease which strikes at random. There she remains firmly in the great individualistic tradition of the twentieth-century English novel.

A note on the text

I'm the King of the Castle was first published by Hamish Hamilton, London, in 1970, and reissued in the Uniform Edition of Susan Hill in 1980. It was published in paperback by Penguin Books, Harmondsworth, in 1974, and reprinted with an Afterword in 1988, and again in 1989. It was also published in paperback by Longman in Longman Imprint Books in 1981. The Penguin edition has been used in the preparation of these Notes.

Part 2

Summaries
of I'M THE KING OF THE CASTLE

A general summary

After the death of his mother, Mr Joseph Hooper, a widower with a ten-year-old son, Edmund, returns to his father's house, Warings. He had left the house some years before, following a quarrel with his father. When his father too dies, Mr Hooper becomes the master of the house. Out of a growing respect for family tradition he had taken Edmund to see his dying grandfather but the visit was not a success. The old man was unconscious and therefore unaware of their presence, and Edmund remained unmoved by the occasion, impressed only by the resemblance between his grandfather and the moths which he had collected.

Edmund is forbidden to go into the Red Room which houses his grandfather's collection of moths, but having found out where his father keeps the key to the room, he is able to enter the room when his father is asleep. He touches a large Death's Head moth which crumbles into dust.

Mr Hooper is uneasy about his son, about his secretive, hard, cold nature, very like his dead mother's; he feels the need to make changes, to improve his way of life. He engages a housekeeper, Mrs Helena Kingshaw, a widow with a son of Edmund's age, Charles. Edmund is furious at this intrusion. He refuses to meet the Kingshaws when they arrive, and throws down a message to the boy Charles, telling him that he is not wanted.

The newcomer is willing to be friendly, but when Edmund mocks him for being poor, Charles strikes him and they fight. Mr Hooper reproves Edmund for his unfriendly behaviour to Charles, and Edmund's resentment grows stronger still.

Charles is unhappy in the house, oppressed by Edmund's dislike. He takes a walk in the fields behind the house, and is pursued and attacked by a huge crow. Badly shaken by the incident he returns to the house only to be mocked by Edmund who had watched him from his bedroom.

Edmund's inventiveness in inflicting misery on Charles is remarkable. He finds a stuffed crow in the attic and places it on Charles's bed during the night. Charles wakes and sees the crow, but manages to remain silent and not to shout for help. In the morning Edmund removes the crow in Charles's absence, and neither of the boys makes any reference to the incident.

Edmund takes Charles to see the collection in the Red Room, sensing Charles's horror of moths. He locks Charles in the room, and when the grown-ups find him and release him, Charles pretends that he had been locked in by mistake. His misery, however, is so great that he decides to run away. He makes his plans very carefully, collecting gradually all the things he might need. Edmund has been watching him, though, and guesses what Charles's plans are.

Charles's opportunity comes when he hears that his mother is going to London with Mr Hooper to do some shopping for a cocktail party which Mr Hooper is planning to give, and will not notice her son's absence until late in the evening when she returns. Charles leaves the house very early in the morning and makes his way to Hang Wood, the wood beyond the fields behind the house, as he feels sure that it would not occur to anyone to look for him there.

He is frightened at first, and has to force himself to leave the open field for the dense wood, but once inside the wood he feels oddly safe. His feeling of security is short-lived, however. Edmund had followed him into the wood and has now caught up with him. To Charles it seems strangely inevitable that he should not be able to escape from Edmund, to rid himself of his fear of him.

The boys lose their way in the wood when they follow a deer, and both are afraid now. A storm breaks out, and Edmund is hysterical with terror. Charles tries to comfort him, and feels reassured by this evidence of human weakness in his enemy. When the storm is over, however, Edmund resumes his former position as leader. The boys find a stream and follow it, arriving eventually at a clearing with a pool. They swim in the pool, enjoying the bathe, but by and by they begin to feel cold. They build a fire and Charles decides to explore the wood for a possible way out, using a ball of string to guide him back. He fails to find a path and returns to the clearing only to find Edmund unconscious, lying down the bank of the pool. He had been trying to catch a fish and slipped, hitting his head on a stone. Charles pulls him out and makes a clumsy but eventually successful attempt to revive him. They sit by the fire, bickering; Edmund is frightened and weeps hysterically till they both fall asleep. In the morning the search party sent to look for them arrives.

When they return to the house, Edmund accuses Charles of pushing him into the water, having forced him to accompany him to the wood. Charles, incoherent with indignation and anger, tries to tell the grown-ups what had really happened but realises that they do not believe him. He screams in helpless rage and is sent to his room. Later his mother comes to see him but though she speaks kindly to him it is clear that she still does not believe his version of the events.

Next morning Charles is told that he will not be going back to his old school (where he was a charity pupil) after the holidays, but will be joining Edmund at his school, at Mr Hooper's expense. Shattered, he runs out of the house and hides in the garden shed. Edmund locks him in, knowing that Charles will be frightened in the dark. Worn out with terror Charles falls asleep. Lost in a nightmare he is woken up by Edmund's voice outside. Edmund mocks him and threatens to make his life a misery at the new school. Charles screams in distress; then, suddenly, Edmund unlocks the door.

In the afternoon all four go on an outing to the ruins of Leydell Castle. Charles, who has no fear of heights, climbs high up the wall of the ruined castle, and Edmund tries to follow. He loses his nerve, and when Charles reaches out to help him, Edmund flinches and falls. He is taken away in an ambulance, and Charles returns to Warings with his mother and Mr Hooper. He assumes that Edmund is dead and tries to explain that the accident was not his fault, but again the grown-ups do not believe him. In the night he has a nightmare and runs out of his room sobbing and calling for his mother. Mr Hooper takes him downstairs where his mother comforts him, and Mr Hooper carries him back to bed. Only now does Charles discover that Edmund is alive and that his injuries are not serious.

Charles goes to the village church to ask God's forgiveness because he did wish Edmund to die. He meets a boy in the church, Fielding, the son of a local farmer. They play together and soon are friends. Charles talks to his new friend about Edmund, but Fielding, though kind and trying to comfort him, cannot understand the hold Edmund has over him.

When Edmund returns from hospital, the relationship between the two boys worsens, as Mrs Kingshaw cossets Edmund and tries to make Charles stay with him. Charles is taken to London by Mr Hooper to buy his uniform for the new school. When he returns he finds that his mother has given Edmund his model of a helter-skelter which he had made himself and of which he is very proud. Beside himself with rage, Charles rushes to Edmund's room to take the model from him, and Edmund throws it across the room, breaking it.

Mr Hooper decides to ask Mrs Kingshaw to marry him, but first he will take them all on another outing. They go to a circus, which Charles hates because he cannot bear to watch the humiliation of the trained animals. His misery is great, and on the way out he is violently sick.

Mrs Kingshaw has invited Fielding to tea, and Charles feels that now he has lost the last thing that was his only, his friendship with Fielding. He is angry and refuses to join the other two in play, though he observes the failure of Edmund's attempts to intimidate his friend. He feels that he is completely alone now, and wants to be left alone. He leaves the other two and goes to Edmund's room, removes the battle charts and lists of regiments on which Edmund has been working, takes them to a clearing near the house and burns them all. He is frightened now, waiting for Edmund's revenge.

The house is busy with preparations as Mr Hooper and Mrs Kingshaw plan to get married on the day the boys are due back at school. They will all drive down to the school after the wedding lunch, and the parents will leave when the boys are settled in.

In the night Edmund pushes a sheet of paper under Charles's door, saying just 'Something will happen to you, Kingshaw.' Charles is terrified, but when he wakes up in the morning he knows what he has to do. He leaves the house early, returns to the pool in the clearing in Hang Wood, undresses, and lies face down in the water. When he is missed at the house, Edmund knows at once where to look for him. When he sees Charles's dead body in the water, Edmund feels triumphant: he, and he alone, has caused this to happen.

Detailed summaries

Chapter 1

The first chapter establishes in an indirect and complex fashion, changing from the thoughts of one person to those of another, two of the main characters: Joseph Hooper, a widower, and his ten-year-old son Edmund. They have come to live at Warings, the family house, after the death of Joseph Hooper's mother. His father, with whom he had quarrelled bitterly, has suffered two strokes and is dying. Edmund was taken by his father to see his dying grandfather, but the old man was unconscious and quite unaware of their presence. Joseph Hooper is painfully aware of the long estrangement between himself and his father, and is also vaguely conscious of the lack of communication or any affection between himself and his son. After his father's death Joseph Hooper inherits the family property.

He has vague plans for improving his unsatisfactory relationship with his son, for 'doing something about it', but at the same time he has no real interest in the boy and knows nothing about him. (He suggests, for example, that the boy should be out playing cricket, even though he has no friends with whom he could play.) It is plain also that he has no liking or love for his son, and his son cares nothing for his father. He is a self-possessed, cool, secretive child, with no warmth of affection for anyone. The visit to his grandfather's deathbed failed to move him, though he was interested in the old man's extraordinary resemblance to the moths which he had collected all his life.

Joseph Hooper has no interest in his father's collection either; like Edmund he values it as a family possession. He forbids the boy to enter the Red Room in which the cases of moths are kept. Edmund takes the key to the room during the night when his father is asleep, and inspects the collection. When he tries to remove a large Death's Head moth from one of the cases, the moth crumbles into dry dust, a symbol perhaps of the uselessness of the whole collection.

NOTES AND GLOSSARY:

stroke: paralysis caused by bleeding in the brain

a dynastic sense: an awareness of the importance of the family, of the need to ensure that it continues, passing on its values and its possessions from father to son

paraphernalia: trappings, various accompaniments

May: a pedantic insistence on correct English: 'Can I' means 'am I able to', while 'May I' means 'am I allowed to'

like an old busy port which has been deserted by the sea: there are such ports (for instance, Rye and Winchelsea in Sussex) which have lost their importance and indeed their livelihood when their harbours became silted up, no longer allowing shipping access to them. Such towns can have a melancholy, forsaken air

rising in the world: becoming rich and important in society

baronet: the lowest rank of hereditary title

with no margin: using up all his money, saving nothing

knowingness: sly cleverness

graceless: lacking gracefulness, plain and clumsy

drive: path to a house wide enough for carriages and cars

everything was predictable: the decor and the furnishings were such as one would expect in an old house of this size

prepossessing: making a favourable impression (the word is much more common in its negative form, 'unprepossessing')

ineffectual: weak

little regarded: not respected much

copse: small wood

on his landing: in the level passage outside his room

Banker's Journal ... Stockbroker's Gazette: professional journals for people who work in banks or buy and sell shares on the stock market

lepidopterist: student of butterflies and moths

removed from their poison-fume bottles: insects intended for collections were killed by poison fumes so that their bodies, and especially their wings, remained undamaged

larvae: caterpillars

Hawk Moths: so called because their flight resembles the darting and hovering of a hawk

Footmen Moths: moths of the family Lithsiidae

Lutestring Moths: named after marks on their wings which resemble the strings of a lute

stilted: stiff, unnatural

Acheroptia atropos: Latin name for the Death's Head moth which has marks like a skull on the back of its body

Chapter 2

Joseph Hooper decides to engage a housekeeper. His advertisement is answered by Mrs Helena Kingshaw, a widow with a son of Edmund's age, Charles. Joseph Hooper likes her letter and engages her on a trial basis. Edmund is furious at this intrusion into his solitude, and hides at first to avoid greeting the new arrivals, sending a message to Charles instead, telling him that he is not wanted.

When the two boys meet, they talk briefly and then fight. Edmund finds it easy to establish superiority over Charles, a quiet, frightened boy, painfully aware of his insecure position in life. Edmund mocks him for being poor, for not having a house of his own. Charles has been prepared for a compromise, ready even to admit the other boy's superiority, but Edmund's hostility, the irrational hatred he displays, confuses Charles. Edmund is rebuked by his father for being unfriendly to the newcomer, for staying in his room. He answers insolently and his father retreats baffled. Edmund then decides to pretend to obey his father and show Charles round the house, mocking him the while. Charles feels a sudden blind desire to push his tormentor down the stairwell, but instead he sits quietly, miserable.

NOTES AND GLOSSARY:

rub along: live together in reasonable harmony
cheval mirror: full-length mirror on a stand
barrow: prehistoric grave mound
Battle of Waterloo map: map of the land battle fought in 1815, in which Wellington defeated Napolean
the Battle of Britain: prolonged air attack by the German Luftwaffe to destroy the RAF (August–October 1940), in which the RAF Fighter Command was victorious
cadaverous: pale, like a corpse
brought up sharp: stopped sharply
the answer to a prayer: the way out of a difficult situation
supercilious: mockingly superior in manner

Chapter 3

Charles decides to get away from Edmund and explore the land beyond the house. There is a copse skirting the fields that run up to Hang Wood, a wood following the top of a ridge, and beyond there is a forest. It is a hot day, and Charles decides to avoid the dark copse and walk instead across the cornfield. Halfway across the field he notices a huge crow circling overhead. The bird dives, almost attacking him. Charles starts running back, pursued by the monstrous bird. He panics and falls, and the bird swoops down on him, landing on his back. Charles's screams scare the bird off. The whole scene is watched by Edmund from his bedroom window. He mocks Charles for his cowardice, and is excited by the power he has over his enemy.

Edmund thinks of another way to torture Charles: he finds a stuffed crow in the attic and in the middle of the night he puts it on Charles's bed. The boy wakes, puts his light on and at once realises what has happened, but cannot bring himself to push the horrible stuffed bird off his bed. It lies there until the morning when Edmund removes it while Charles is in the bathroom. At breakfast neither of the boys mentions the incident. Edmund watches Charles taking a toy submarine out of a cereal packet and tells him condescendingly that he may keep it. Charles looks at him with hate and leaves the toy on the table. Edmund offers to show him the Red Room in the evening.

Charles does not dare to refuse the invitation, despite the fact that the room terrifies him as he has always been frightened of moths. Once Charles is inside the room, Edmund runs out, locking him in. Charles is rescued later in the evening by his mother and Mr Hooper, and pretends that he had been locked in by mistake. In his room he thinks of his school, the only place where he feels safe.

NOTES AND GLOSSARY:

scrubland:	uncultivated land covered with coarse grass and small bushes
Keck:	a dialect word for any plant of the Umbelliferae family, with tall hollow stems and large leaves
sorrel:	tall plant with sour-tasting reddish-green leaves; all the plants here are of a harsh, unpleasant nature, hostile like the house itself
stone-walling:	silent resistance
Stare you out:	look at you fixedly to force you to blink and look away
a galleon model:	a model of a sailing ship
catacombs:	underground burial-places

Chapter 4

One day Edmund goes to London with his father, and Charles, left free to roam about the house, discovers a small attic room which he likes. It has a lock on the door, and he feels safe there. Meanwhile Mr Hooper tries to talk to Edmund on the way back from London, asking him to behave in a friendlier way towards Charles, who is fatherless. Edmund, motherless, looks at his father coldly. Mr Hooper, remembering his dislike of his own father, tells himself that he cannot be blamed for his failure to make contact with Edmund. Though he is uneasy about his relationship with his son, he has no idea at all of what goes on in the boy's mind.

Charles uses his newly found room to make his preparations to run away. As always he is realistic about his chances and is prepared to fail. He knows, however, that even if he fails the very act of his running away will be enough to make the grown-ups realise his distress.

It is raining, and Mr Hooper orders the boys to play bagatelle together. Against the grown-ups' self-congratulatory remarks about the boys' growing friendship, Charles and Edmund play the game fiercely, willing each other to lose.

Edmund finds out about Charles's room and, having inspected his hoard of provisions, he has guessed what Charles is planning to do. He feels triumphant at driving Charles away and declares that he will come too.

In an ironic counterpoint to Charles's desperate plan, Mr Hooper has plans of his own – he will have the house redecorated, throw out the lumber from the attics and even give a Sunday morning cocktail party to mark his taking over the house. Mrs Kingshaw, pleased and excited, joins in his plans.

NOTES AND GLOSSARY:

exonerated: freed from guilt

mew yourselves up: shut yourselves indoors

a lark: a frolic, a mischievous adventure

bagatelle: a game in which steel balls are shot on to a board with holes in it. The object is to make these balls settle in the holes, each of which carries a different number of points. The highest scorer wins

unresourceful: unable to think of something to do

footling: unimportant, silly

there were a lot more things, worse things: the reader is left to guess what these things are – perhaps the change in Mrs Kingshaw who is clearly hoping to marry Mr Hooper, or the dark sinister house in which Charles now sees himself as imprisoned, or perhaps his hatred of Edmund which frightens Charles

taken a load off my shoulders: relieved me from worry

Chapter 5

Mrs Kingshaw is going to London with Mr Hooper to do some shopping for the planned cocktail party. Charles decides that the best time to run away is early on the morning of their departure when with any luck his absence will not be noticed until the evening. He puts some food and other necessities into a satchel and sets his alarm clock very early. He is awake before his alarm rings, and lies in bed thinking about his mother, how ignorant she is about his misery, imagining that he is settling down nicely.

When it is time, he gets dressed and slips out of the house, making for the cornfield and for Hang Wood beyond. He feels sure that no one will look for him there because Edmund knows how frightened he is of the wood. As he makes his way through the morning mist he remembers his encounter with the crow and is afraid, but he is excited too, proud of how well he had planned his escape and how well he is managing. He notices, however, a wart on his finger which he believes had been wished on him by a boy at his school, to get rid of his own warts. This frightens him as evidence of ill-will and a sign of bad luck. He has some difficulty in getting inside the wood which is surrounded by a thick hedge and barbed wire, but after a while he finds a gap, shuts his eyes and makes himself jump inside the wood.

NOTES AND GLOSSARY:

a stir: a sensation, an excitement
tussocky: growing in clumps
docks: tall plants with large leaves
doubloons: old Spanish gold coins
beaded cobwebs: cobwebs with drops of dew or mist on them
like something left on the moon landscape: Susan Hill started this novel during the summer of 1969 when the American astronauts landed on the moon and left a lot of debris there, a fact which struck many people as ironic and memorable
letting himself off: permitting himself to avoid going through the wood because he was frightened of it
ragged: made fun of

Chapter 6

Once inside the wood Charles is happy. He feels safe there, completely hidden. He sits down, watches a rabbit and has some food. He is thirsty now, but he has no water as he thought that a water bottle would be too heavy to carry. He moves further into the wood and then suddenly he hears a noise. Something is approaching. He hides behind a bush, and then the trees part and Edmund comes towards him. He too has a satchel and has clearly been following Charles. Charles feels no surprise: it seems inevitable that Edmund would come too.

Edmund mocks him for his stupidity in choosing such an obvious day for running away, when the grown-ups are to be away. He himself only had to watch from his bedroom and then follow. He declares that he can please himself in following Charles because Charles's mother is only a servant in his own father's house. Charles turns away and goes on into the wood, with Edmund following.

The wood is very dense now, and suddenly they hear a strange honking noise. Charles is frightened but suddenly he realises that Edmund is frightened too, that he too is human, sweating and afraid. The noise turns out to be the call of a deer, and the boys follow it, hoping that it will lead them to a whole herd. For a while they play at hunters, but Charles is aware of time passing, and he wants to get out of the wood. Suddenly he realises that they are lost. The air is hot and still, and in the distance the first distant rumble of thunder is heard.

NOTES AND GLOSSARY:

soughing:	sighing like the wind
moleskin:	heavy cotton cloth with a smooth surface
groin:	here, a place where a branch joins the tree-trunk
it was all quite all right:	the phrase has evidently a special meaning for Charles – it was safe, unthreatening
clearing:	open place in a wood
aqueous:	watery
flail out:	hit out wildly with his arms
get his bearings:	identify his position and the direction in which to go
crumpled:	collapsed

Chapter 7

The storm is coming closer, and Charles realises that Edmund is in a state of blind panic. Charles himself is not afraid at all; he rigs up a shelter for them both with his anorak, and while the storm rages overhead he watches Edmund whimpering and moaning, beside himself with terror. Once the storm is over, Edmund recovers and takes up the leader's position once more. Charles had expected that having been observed succumbing to panic Edmund would feel that their relationship had changed, but clearly this is not so, and Charles submits. They are both thirsty now, and decide to search for the stream which they can hear somewhere in the distance. On the way Charles finds a dead rabbit, and Edmund's remarks on it, which apply to dead people as well ('When you're dead, you're dead, you're finished'), in their matter-of-factness and total lack of sympathy bring home to Charles the difference between them. Edmund has no pity because he has no love.

They reach the stream and decide to follow it, hoping that it will lead them out of the wood. The way is difficult and unpleasant, and Edmund wants to go back, but Charles refuses and Edmund has to follow. They come out into a clearing where the stream has made a pool, and they bathe. Charles hesitates at first, remembering his terror of the swimming-pool when he was small, but then he leaps in. The bathe is delightful, and they play in the water until the sun goes in. Once the sun has gone they both suddenly feel very cold. Charles decides to build a fire, but Edmund refuses to join in the work, fearful of losing his mastery over Charles. Charles realises that the difference between them lies in the nature of their fears. Edmund is only afraid of external events over which he has no control, like the thunderstorm, but which will come to an end leaving him unafraid once more, while Charles's fears come from within him, and can be reawakened any time.

In the end they build the fire together and while they are working they discuss their situation. Edmund suggests that without realising it they have gone through Hang Wood, which after all is not very big, into the adjoining vast Barnard Forest. Talking about it Edmund succumbs to an attack of panic. Charles finds his hysterical screams intolerable and he slaps him. Edmund stops screaming, sobs for a while and then vomits.

Charles has thought of a way of ascertaining their position without getting lost. Like Theseus in the Greek legend he will use the ball of string which he had packed with his other belongings in the satchel, to walk forward to try to find a way. Edmund does not like the idea but Charles persists. He walks a long way and catches a rabbit, but cannot bring himself to kill it. He likes the solitude of the wood and is tempted to go on walking, leaving Edmund behind, but his conscience will not let him.

He returns to the clearing where he finds Edmund lying face down just above the water level, unconscious from a wound on his forehead. He had hit it on a stone when he was trying to catch a fish. Charles manages to pull him out, and makes a clumsy attempt to restore his breathing. He is successful and Edmund recovers. Charles lights a fire to make a hot drink for Edmund. While busying himself with the fire Edmund asks him if he has found a way out of the wood, saying that if Charles tries to leave on his own he will kill him. Charles tells Edmund that he has not found a way out of the wood.

NOTES AND GLOSSARY:

vindictive: liking to revenge himself
guff: nonsense
grubs: thick soft insect larvae
Somebody did that once in history: Charles is remembering the Greek legend of Theseus who killed the Minotaur, a monster with the body of a man and the head of a bull, in the labyrinth of the Cretan king Minos. Theseus was helped by the king's daughter, Ariadne, who gave

him a ball of thread so that he could find his way
back out of the labyrinth. Theseus took Ariadne with
him on leaving the island, only to desert her later

Chapter 8

It is getting dark, and the boys are sitting by the fire, talking. Edmund
boasts of the expensive watch his father has promised him for Christmas.
Charles has caught a fish but cannot bring himself to kill it and leaves it on
the grass to die. He tries to cook it, but his attempt is not successful and
the fish is quite inedible. Edmund speculates on how soon it will be before
the grown-ups discover their absence, and he mocks Charles because his
mother usually comes up to his bedroom to say goodnight to him. Intent
on wounding Charles further, he asks how often his mother has tried to
catch a husband before, as she is now trying to catch his father. Charles is
furious, yet he feels the truth of the accusation, and finds himself hating
his mother for it.

It is night now, and Charles sits up by the fire, listening to the night
animals. Edmund has a nightmare and screams hysterically. Charles finds
himself hitting him again. Edmund wakes up, frightened, blaming Charles
for their predicament. He declares that when they are found he will accuse
Charles of having forced him to come with him. Charles feels that he
wants to hit Edmund again but stops himself. He promises not to leave
Edmund who is clearly ill after his fall, and comforts him. He knows that
Edmund will use any weakness of his against him, yet he feels that he
himself has some inner strength that will help him so that he no longer
needs to run away.

NOTES AND GLOSSARY:
glutinous: sticky
gone after a lot of people: tried to attract many men
those boys' prison places: Edmund means Borstals, detention centres for
juvenile delinquents, named after the first of them, at
Borstal near Rochester in Kent

Chapter 9

In the morning Edmund is better, though he has a dark bruise on his
forehead. Charles decides to go for a swim in the pool and, lying in the
water, he feels happy and safe. At this point he hears voices and dogs
barking. The searchers have found them, and he feels frightened at the
thought of having to go back to the house, but he remembers all that had
happened in the wood, and hopes that his relationship with Edmund has
changed.

NOTES AND GLOSSARY:
watered silk: silk marked with a wavy pattern
They fidgeted gently: the leaves moved continuously as if impatient

Chapter 10

When they are back at the house Edmund accuses Charles of having pushed him into the water so that he hit his head and of manhandling him afterwards. (This is true in a way, of course, but is a distorted version of Charles's efforts to carry out artificial respiration.) Charles tries to defend himself against this monstrous accusation but realises the uselessness of it as clearly neither Mr Hooper nor his mother believes him. In his frantic attempt to defend himself he shouts, abusing Edmund, unable to articulate all that he has done for him.

He is sent upstairs in disgrace, and feels trapped by the house, helpless against Edmund's lying and bullying. He is aware that he is behaving in a way which is quite unlike him, that the situation in which he finds himself is changing him. He lies down on his bed, dozes off, and is awakened by his mother who has come to talk to him. As she talks it becomes increasingly clear that she has no conception at all of the nature of the relationship between the two boys, her soothing clichés standing in stark contrast to the misery of her son's life. She tells him that there is something she wants to tell him, but that she will keep it until the next day as a lovely surprise.

After she has gone, Charles lies thinking. He is sure that his mother is going to tell him that she and Mr Hooper are getting married, which will make escape from the house and from Edmund quite impossible. He thinks of the wood which may have frightened him, yet made him feel safer because 'people are no good . . . There are only things and places.'

NOTES AND GLOSSARY:
Thank you for my drink: Charles's formal words imply that he now
regards his mother as a stranger
perhaps Edmund is not quite like all your other friends: even
Mrs Kingshaw, who is not perceptive as a rule, seems
to be aware that there is something odd about
Edmund

Chapter 11

The next morning at breakfast Charles hears the news: he is not going back to his school in Wales; instead he will be joining Edmund at his school. The news is so awful, so shattering that he feels he must get away from Edmund at once. He would like to go back to the wood, to the clearing with the stream, but he knows that Edmund would find him there. Instead he runs across the garden and hides in the garden shed. As soon as he is inside the shed he hears the door slam and the padlock clicks shut. He knows that Edmund has locked him in. He is frightened in the dark and sick with terror. In the end worn out with fear he falls asleep. He has a nightmare of going to a Punch and Judy show with other boys from his school, and seeing the puppets turn human, and bleed profusely when hit. The stage fills with crows which rise above the boys' heads. At this point he wakes and hears Edmund calling him mockingly, telling him that he will not be found.

The torture goes on: Edmund promises that he will turn the other boys at school against him and make his life unbearable. Then he turns to Charles's fear of moths and tells him that he will have to dissect dead moths at school, that there are moths, rats and bats in the shed, till Charles screams with terror and huddles down weeping. Just as lunch is served, Edmund unlocks the door and runs back to the house, telling Mrs Kingshaw that they have been playing at bandits. Charles follows him slowly to the house.

NOTES AND GLOSSARY:

blithe: gay and happy

a scissor of daylight: a sharp, clear image of a narrow shaft of light

the bogs: (*slang*) lavatories

a Punch and Judy show: a puppet show with the traditional characters of Mr Punch, a clown, and his wife Judy. There is always a lot of fighting between Punch and Judy in these shows

like the dust on the surface of the moon: another reminder that the moon was very much in people's minds in 1969, after the American moon landing

dorm: (*slang*) dormitory, bedroom for a group of children at a boarding-school

newers: (*school slang*) new pupils

Chapter 12

Mr Hooper has arranged an outing for the four of them, a drive to the ruins of Leydell Castle. He and Mrs Kingshaw sit talking on a bench by the lake below the castle while the boys explore the ruins. Charles climbs high up the wall of the castle, moving carefully and confidently. This is something he can do well, as he has an excellent head for heights, and he enjoys the achievement. Looking down he realises that Edmund is afraid of heights and dares him to follow. Edmund, furious, starts climbing after him, but some distance below Charles he loses his nerve and refuses to move from the ledge where he is standing. His terror is so great that he wets himself. Charles tries to persuade him to move, as he is blocking Charles's way down. For a moment Charles, knowing that they are unobserved by the grown-ups, is tempted to push Edmund off the ledge, but he knows that he cannot do it. He decides to take hold of Edmund's hand to guide him down, but Edmund misreads the movement of his hand and backs away, loses his footing and falls.

NOTES AND GLOSSARY:

The rain had come to nothing: it hardly rained at all

by halves: imperfectly

bowman: archer, soldier armed with a bow and arrows

I'm the King of the Castle: the children's rhyme 'I'm the king of the castle, and you're a dirty rascal' provides the title of the novel and sums up its main theme: the struggle between the two boys, with Edmund trying to break Charles and frighten him into submission while Charles is fighting desperately to hold on to his identity, to find some security. It is perhaps not entirely fanciful to say that the reference to the nursery rhyme is made here to symbolise the fight between good and evil

Chapter 13

Charles watches Edmund falling, and it seems to take a long time before he hits the ground. Mr Hooper and Mrs Kingshaw come running, other people appear, and an ambulance arrives and takes Edmund away. Charles's mother calls him and he climbs down slowly.

They return with Mr Hooper to Warings. Charles thinks that Edmund has been killed, and he remembers a sentence which a senior boy, Lesage, read out in assembly. He thinks of Lesage who used to send him on meaningless errands, and once made him lie on the floor. Charles thought he was going to be beaten, but Lesage just stood there, looking down at him. Charles is too young to grasp the possible sexual implications of the older boy's behaviour, but even remembering the incident disturbs him. He tries to explain to his mother that the accident was not his fault, that Edmund alone was to be blamed for trying to follow him when he must have known that he should not climb becuase he was frightened of heights. His mother does not seem to understand, but she begs Charles to promise to be more sensible in the future. Her voice betrays only her fear at what might have happened, and there is no warmth of love in it. She goes to the hospital, and Charles watches television with Mrs Boland, the daily help. The scenes of violence on the screen frighten him, and he moves away. He goes to his room quickly when told to go to bed, and lies in bed imagining what his life will be like now, with Edmund dead. He will be free of him, he will be able to go back to his old school, he will now be the King of the Castle.

He falls asleep and has another nightmare, again dreaming of the puppets and the crows. Running away from them he finds himself falling from a great height. He wakes up crying and, losing his usual self-control, he runs sobbing to his mother's bedroom but finds it empty. Mrs Kingshaw and Mr Hooper have by now returned from the hospital and are sitting downstairs, talking. Mr Hooper carries Charles down into the sitting-room, and he is comforted and given a hot drink. Only when he tries to explain that his nightmare was caused by Edmund's death does he learn that Edmund is alive. Mr Hooper carries Charles back to bed, and Charles is ashamed that he likes being comforted and carried by him. In the night he wakes up again, remembering that Edmund is not dead.

NOTES AND GLOSSARY:

a rumble of thunder: there is perhaps an echo here of the events in the wood when Edmund broke down and Charles was in charge

Prep: (*school slang*) preparation of lessons, homework

a King's Scholarship: these scholarships (there are 70 of them) were established by the founder of Eton College (which dates from 1440), King Henry VI

A combine harvester rolled down a field like a dinosaur: the reader may recall Charles sitting on a tractor on his way to Hang Wood (Chapter 5) where the machine was compared to a great beast. The clumsy movements of agricultural machinery do indeed resemble those of a huge beast

looking down into the white, white sink: the repetition of the adjective, which has the effect of stressing the whiteness of the sink, shows how intensely Charles is aware of his surroundings. This is common in moments of stress when the mind seems to seize on a small detail to avoid realising fully whatever has caused the stress. This part of the narrative, which describes Charles's anguished state, is full of small visual details

The palm of it was very dry and hard: the hardness and dryness recall a bird's claw, and the reader may remember that in Chapter 10 Mr Hooper is described as 'very tall and thin and grey, like some sort of terrible bird'. The description links Mr Hooper with the crow, one of the menacing symbols in the novel

his long, thin legs, opening like scissors: the same image is used in Chapter 9 ('opened his legs wide and then closed them, like scissors')

Chapter 14

One day Mr Hooper has to go to London, and Mrs Kingshaw is going to the hospital to visit Edmund, leaving Charles with Mrs Boland. Before she leaves, Mrs Kingshaw suggests that Charles should send Edmund a kind message or perhaps buy him a present. Charles refuses, furious, and tries to make his mother understand how much he hates Edmund. He remembers Mr Hooper carrying him and feels ashamed, thinking of Fenwick, a boy at his school who bore pain bravely when he had a bad fall. Charles has been left on his own a lot at this time, and he makes a successful working model of a helter-skelter of which he is very proud.

Left alone in the house again, Charles plays with Edmund's jigsaw, then goes to the church in the neighbouring village, Derne, and kneels down in the chancel to pray, asking God to forgive him for wishing Edmund dead and not to punish him for such a terrible wish. A boy speaks to him who seems to know him by sight. They talk a little and play, getting on very well together. The boy, Fielding, invites Charles to his house to see a calving cow and some baby turkeys. Charles watches the birth of the calf, half-horrified and half-fascinated. He feels sorry for the turkeys who are all going to be slaughtered at Christmas. Fielding seems to understand Charles's distress, though, being country-born, he does not share it. However, he does not laugh at Charles for being soft-hearted, as Edmund would.

Charles is invited to stay for dinner and goes back to Warings to ask for permission to stay. His mother is there, back from the hospital, and tells him that Edmund will be back the next day. Shattered by this news, Charles talks to Fielding about Edmund, but finds it impossible to explain the hold that Edmund has over him. Fielding, though a kind-hearted boy, is too practical and sensible to understand Charles's terrors, telling him that he will find new friends at Edmund's school and that Edmund will not be able to spoil everything for him. Charles knows that this is not how things will be, but he is cheered and encouraged nevertheless. The next day Charles learns that Edmund will not be coming home yet, and he is wild with delight and hope.

NOTES AND GLOSSARY:

The quad: the quadrangle, a square piece of ground with buildings round all four sides

the San: the sanatorium, room reserved for sick pupils

Form: the class the boys belong to

brazened it out:	made people accept him by his impudence
helter-skelter:	fairground spiral slide
gargoyles:	waterspouts for taking away rainwater from a roof, usually carved in the shape of grotesque animal or human heads
chancel:	eastern part of a church, usually reserved for the clergy
plantains:	plants with spikes of small flowers on long stems
mesmerized:	fascinated, as if under hypnosis
mucus:	slimy liquid produced in some parts of the body
Heifer:	young cow

Kingshaw's eyes pricked: Charles has a deep intuitive sympathy with animals, and he wants to cry

that is how you ought to be: Fielding's mother is the sort of person Charles wishes his own mother to be

goldcrest:	very small singing-bird
slow-worm:	a harmless snake-like legless lizard
let-down:	disappointed

Chapter 15

Edmund has come home and seems to know at once that Charles has been to his room and borrowed his jigsaw. He calls Charles a thief and the boys bicker, the dislike they feel for one another egging them on. Edmund accuses Charles of having pushed him off the castle wall, but Charles hardly bothers to defend himself. Edmund threatens him with punishment for this: 'Something will happen to you. You wait.' Charles accepts this – like most children he believes in divine punishment for thinking bad thoughts. He thinks of what will happen to him at Edmund's school, and remembers the time when a bully named Crawford at his old school had beaten him up.

Edmund still has to stay in bed, and Charles's mother orders her son to keep Edmund company. Charles feels that her attitude towards him has changed, that she has become impatient and hard with him, and he feels that she is acting in this way to please Mr Hooper.

He slips out to the village, ostensibly to buy an ice-cream, and meets Fielding who is driving with his father to market with new-born calves. Charles will not come with them because he does not want to ask for permission at the house, and also he is afraid of the painful scenes he would see at the cattle market.

He goes back to Warings, and is sent up to Edmund's room. Edmund tells him that he knows all about Fielding, that Charles's mother has told him. Charles feels betrayed; now he has nothing that is all his own. Also, he is jealous because his mother has been paying more attention to

Edmund than to himself. His jealous feelings have surprised him because he feels in his own heart that he has no love for his mother.

The next day he is taken by Mr Hooper to London to buy the uniform for his new school. Mr Hooper finds him much easier to deal with than his own son. Since Mrs Kingshaw's arrival he has been feeling more confident in every way, sure that he knows how to deal with the boys: all they need is a firm hand (he has conveniently forgotten the miseries of his own unhappy childhood, and regards it as a simple, happy time).

When they return to the house Charles finds that during his absence his mother has given his model of the helter-skelter to Edmund. He rushes blindly into the sitting-room, shrieking in his rage, and is slapped by Mr Hooper and sent upstairs. He goes straight to Edmund's room and demands the return of his model. Edmund throws it across the room, and it breaks. Mrs Kingshaw reproves Charles for what has happened.

NOTES AND GLOSSARY:

concussion: the shock caused by a violent blow on the head

a party to her secrets: a person with knowledge of her secrets

---

Chapter 16

Mr Hooper overhears Mrs Kingshaw talking to an old friend on the telephone and telling her that she is unsure of her future plans and that she and Charles might be moving again. Mrs Kingshaw knows that he is listening and is really saying it for his benefit, to show him that she has retained her independence and that he cannot be sure that she is his for the asking. Charles overhears her too, and is uncertain about what his mother's words mean. He wonders where they might be going, and he remembers the worst place of all, a private hotel in London. He hated it, because it was so different from other boys' homes, and also because of Miss Mellitt, a lonely old woman who was a permanent resident in the hotel and who was always trying to talk to him. Charles found her physically repulsive and was frightened of her.

Having overheard the telephone conversation as he was meant to, Mr Hooper now makes up his mind to ask Mrs Kingshaw to marry him. He thinks of his unhappy first marriage, of his cold, sexually unresponsive wife, of the lonely years of frustrated sexual desire both before and after her death, and he feels sure that Mrs Kingshaw would respond to his demands.

Edmund tells Charles about the wedding plans, but Charles seems unmoved. He realises that for all his bravado Edmund is upset about the marriage, but he himself feels nothing. Only later, during the night, looking into a future in which Edmund will always be present, does he weep.

A couple of days later all four of them go on a special outing, a surprise arranged by Mr Hooper. This turns out to be a visit to the circus, which Charles has always loathed. The noise and smell terrify him, and he hates to see the humiliation of the performing animals. His mother chooses not to remember this, or at least to make light of it ('But of course all that is quite forgotten, and this is going to be a simply splendid treat.'), and reprimands Charles when he is violently sick after the performance.

Mrs Kingshaw tells Charles that she has gone to the Fieldings' farm and invited Fielding (Anthony, as she calls him) to tea. Charles is angry; having Fielding at Warings, being watched by Edmund, means the end of his own friendship with Fielding, the one thing that he still has.

The wedding has now been settled; it will take place on the morning of the day when the boys are due back at their school. There will be 'a *family* lunch', as Mrs Kingshaw calls it, at the local hotel after the registry wedding, and then they will all go to the school and see the boys settled in. And then, Charles knows, the terror will begin.

Fielding does come to tea and Edmund soon realises that he will not be able to terrorise him. Charles is aware of this and somehow is not at all surprised, though he is painfully conscious of the unfairness of it all. Edmund makes various suggestions for play, all of them intentionally excluding Charles. Fielding is uneasy, aware of the tension, but Charles refuses to respond to his anxious approaches. To him the friendship is now spoiled, and he wants nothing of it. When Edmund goes to the farm with Fielding, Charles goes to Edmund's room, collects the battle charts and lists of regiments on which Edmund has been working, and burns them in a little clearing near the edge of the copse. He knows that Edmund will guess who has taken his charts, and he is afraid.

NOTES AND GLOSSARY:
straws in the wind: signs of possible future developments
arc lights: lamps which use a luminous bridge between two separate carbon poles to create light
heirlooms: valuable objects which have been in the family for generations

Chapter 17

Edmund says nothing about the disappearance of his battle plans and lists, and Charles is all the more frightened by his silence. The house is busy with preparations, the boys' trunks are packed, and Mrs Kingshaw makes ready for the honeymoon at Torquay which will follow the wedding. In the night Charles wakes and finds that a sheet of paper has been pushed under his door. Written on it is just one sentence: 'Something will happen to you, Kingshaw.' Charles is utterly terrified, and his dreams, when he falls asleep, are nightmares.

In the morning he wakes up early and finds that his mind is made up; he knows what to do. Once more he makes his way to the wood, to the clearing with the pool. While Edmund is sleeping a dreamless sleep, his father is tossing about excited by erotic dreams, and Mrs Kingshaw is awake, thinking how well things have turned out, Charles takes off his clothes, folds them in a pile and steps into the water. He hesitates a litle but, remembering all the terrors of the new school and his mother's marriage, he wades into the deepest part of the pool and lies down slowly, face down.

This time there is no difficulty about finding Charles, as Edmund guesses at once where he has gone, and leads the others there. When they arrive at the clearing and see Charles's body in the water, Edmund thinks triumphantly that it has been all his own doing, that Charles has done it because of him. Mrs Kingshaw takes him in her arms and tells him not to look and not to be upset. He hears the splashing as the men wade into the water to take up Charles's body.

NOTES AND GLOSSARY:

the morning reminded him of the time before: it was grey and wet as it had been on the day when he ran away

Mrs Kingshaw thought, there is plenty of time for everything: an ironic thought as presumably none of the things planned for this day will take place

Part 3

Commentary

Structure and technique

If the novel is primarily – and historically, its origins going back to the tales of pre-literate ages – a story which the novelist wants to tell, and which the reader wants to hear, then its structure is the method chosen by the author to tell the story. The first novels, the picaresque tales of the seventeenth century, employed straight chronological form, telling what happened first, and what happened next, and next again. This simple method remained pretty well the only one used throughout the eighteenth and early nineteenth centuries, from Henry Fielding and Tobias Smollett to Jane Austen. Already in the eighteenth century, however, a new way of telling the story was found, in the form of letters (as in Fanny Burney's *Evelina* (1778) or in Samuel Richardson's *Pamela* (1740), *Clarissa* (1747) and *Sir Charles Grandison* (1753)). Generally though, even when no longer employing only the authorial narrative voice and letting the main character tell the tale in letter form, the novel remained a chronological account of events as they took place. (A solitary exception is Laurence Sterne's *Tristram Shandy* (1760) in which eccentricities of typography and style added to interpolations of the past mixed with more recent events, and wilful digressions, challenge the reader's powers of concentration as well as those of understanding.)

Gradually during the nineteenth century the novel changed. With the Romantic interest in landscape, descriptive passages gained an interest they had not possessed before. The emphasis on the individual, on each person's unique thoughts and feelings, brought a subtler, deeper characterisation, and the central character's past, having played its part in moulding his or her nature, grew in importance. What had been largely unknown in earlier novels became a standard feature: a recollection of an illuminating incident from the past came to be used more and more to promote the narrative.

Nowadays this technique, employing a technical term from film-making, is known as the flashback. Even when introduced abruptly and without explanation, it is now understood and interpreted easily by the readers, again perhaps because they are familiar with the device from films.

Susan Hill's novel is a straightforward chronological narrative but the flashback is used frequently, from the very opening words of the novel ('Three months ago, his grandmother died, and then they had moved to this house') which take us to Edmund's first arrival at Warings, establishing the loveless, sombre atmosphere of the house, and Edmund's cold, unemotional response to the visit to his grandfather's deathbed.

The interesting thing about this opening flashback, however, is not just how skilfully it introduces the house and the Hooper family. What is really significant about it – as the reader will come to realise later – is the rare glimpse it offers into Edmund's mind. There are numerous, often quite detailed flashbacks into the past life of the other boy, Charles Kingshaw, telling us about his school, his miserable wandering life with his mother from which his school has become a welcome refuge. We learn from them how Charles taught himself to cope with bullying at school, with his fears, with the dreadful uncertainty of his existence, how he gained his strength of resignation, his low estimate of himself. Through these flashbacks Susan Hill builds up Charles's past history and his character. In an astonishing contrast we learn almost nothing about Edmund Hooper; it is as if his memory were more or less a blank tablet. We know nothing about his life at school or his life at home with his father; the loss of his mother seems to mean little to him. Obviously this is a deliberate omission on the novelist's part: Edmund has almost no memories, no emotional responses to his past and no affections. We might almost say that this is a negative use of the flashback; it is the very absence of this conventional device of the modern novel that draws attention to Edmund's character, as if he were wearing a mask. It may be that the novelist, increasingly aware of the element of evil in the boy's make-up (if we accept the author's implied admission that fictional characters develop a life of their own, independent of the writer), refrained from anything that might bring an understanding of his character and with it a softening of the menace which this incomprehensible character conveys.

We learn more about Edmund's father, a secondary character, who is not without his memories of a loveless childhood and marriage. The flashbacks are few but sufficient to help the reader to understand and, to some extent at least, to pity Mr Hooper.

The past of Mrs Kingshaw, Charles's mother, also remains hidden to us, as she too seems to remember little. There is nothing threatening, however, in the absence of any significant references to her past. She is shallow in her thoughts and feelings, and if she seems reluctant to look back, it is likely that she follows the cosy philosophy of 'What's done is done' and 'No good crying over spilt milk' and looks to the future, always hoping for a turn for the better.

In this way, then, the structure of the novel helps to build up the characters in revealing, or concealing, their past. The action of the novel's present is told mostly through Charles's eyes: what he does, what he sees, what he thinks and feels, and what is done to him. Sometimes the authorial voice tells us what Mr Hooper sees; at times, rarely, we catch a glimpse of

Mrs Kingshaw not as Charles sees her, but as she is, sitting on her bed, smoking, thinking of the future.

Only in the early chapters of the novel are we allowed to enter Edmund's mind, or at least to see the house and its inhabitants through his eyes. He remembers his grandfather's death, he inspects the Red Room, he feels angry at the news of the Kingshaws' impending arrival. But as soon as Charles enters the story Edmund becomes a menacing presence, all the more threatening because his motives remain hidden, incomprehensible (why does he follow Charles into the wood?), and therefore frightening. Again, like the absence of flashbacks into his past, our inability to enter Edmund's mind is a deliberate way of building up and maintaining the incomprehensibility of his character. In the last resort evil remains a mystery to ordinary people, and this is, of course, a part of its power, the helpless incomprehension it arouses in those who come face to face with it.

This, then, is the striking feature of Susan Hill's narrative technique. Basically a chronological account, the novel uses the presence or absence of illuminating flashbacks, the shifting of the viewpoint from which the action is observed, to stress the basic difference between the two protagonists and to build up the feeling of impending disaster. As our incomprehension of Edmund's character and motives grows, so does our unease and with it our sense of danger.

It was said earlier in this section that the novel is a chronological account. To be quite accurate, however, the only narrative passages of any length are those dealing with events which might be described as crisis points in the relationship between the two boys: the crow's attack on Charles and the subsequent incident with the stuffed crow; the boys' wanderings in the wood; Charles's imprisonment in the shed; Edmund's accident in the castle ruins. (Interestingly, these crises do not really affect the relationship: they may strengthen the antagonism, but even the shared dangers in the wood do not bring the boys together. Precisely because nothing can change the hostility between them, and Edmund's domination over Charles, the situation becomes so unbearable that Charles kills himself.) These events apart, however, the narrative does not flow continuously: it consists of incidents, some of them quite brief, linked only by the passage of time that propels them along. We experience them as they are experienced by a child who does not see the pattern of cause and effect linking incidents, but sees only things happening to him or her, often incomprehensibly.

In this way, indirectly, we come to identify with Charles, whose viewpoint predominates, to see incidents as he sees them: disjointed, often meaningless, offering no clues to the future. In other words the form of the narrative continually contributes to our understanding of what Charles is going through, and helps us to gain some conception of his emotional state. This is the technique the author uses to achieve her purpose – to present a series of events in such a way as to make us accept as possible, indeed almost inevitable, the terrible ending; to understand how a young boy could choose suicide. As Susan Hill says in her Afterword, there was 'no other solution, no other way out'. This is how she felt about Charles, and this is how she makes her readers feel too: the technique is a successful means to the novelist's end, to tell a story and make us believe in it absolutely.

Themes

Unless an author sets out with the clear purpose of using a novel to impart a message or to prove the validity of his or her views (the *roman à thèse* of literary categories) the main themes of a novel may not be immediately obvious to the reader. Yet every novel carries within it one or more themes, groupings of thoughts or feelings that have inspired the writing of it, influenced its style and imagery, given it its distinctive character.

In *I'm the King of the Castle* the main themes have been defined for us by the author herself in the Afterword. It is a novel about children; 'about cruelty and the power of evil . . . But most of all it is about isolation and the lack of love.' Another theme, stemming from that of isolation, might be added: people's inability to communicate with one another in any true sense and the failure of language to express feelings. Yet another theme, paralleling the lovelessness of the main characters and their emotional isolation, is Susan Hill's vision of nature as 'red in tooth and claw', indifferent and cruel as human nature itself.

Childhood

As Susan Hill says in her Afterword, *I'm the King of the Castle* is a book about children, but not necessarily for children. Having aimed the book at an adult readership, she was astonished at its success among young people (a success reflected by its becoming a set book for GCSE). Its success seemed to contradict her own view that one cannot really understand childhood until it has become the past, a country only to be viewed with hindsight. It seemed that in her novel she touched a raw nerve, described something that far too many children have experienced for themselves: the helplessness in the face of cruelty, be it ordinary classroom bullying or other, truly pathological manifestations of malice. The classroom debates she mentions presumably centred on whether Charles's suicide was inevitable, whether there were ways in which he could have helped himself, anyone to whom he could have turned. A child's answer to any such questions would be a bleak 'No'. Adults might think of the social services, of other people, perhaps the headmaster of Charles's old school or Fielding's kind mother, but any such solutions, of doubtful effectiveness in any case, simply would not occur to a desperate child.

In this situation the past becomes truly a foreign country (as L. P. Hartley said in his novel *The Go-Between* (1953)) for adults who no longer can understand how things are done in that country of childhood. Adults are outraged at the notion of a child's suicide, yet young readers will see Charles's drowning as a reasonable alternative to a life of endless misery to which *he* can see no end because he is unable truly to envisage the independence of adulthood, which in any case seems hopelessly distant to him.

The theme of childhood in this novel, then, is not one of remembrance, of going back to relive its joys and miseries. It is a theme of present hopelessness, of unendurable misery, which most adults will prefer not to remember too clearly if they have experienced it for themselves, and to which young readers will respond at once, with the strength of their response serving as an indicator both of their own experiences and of the novelist's ability to re-create such experiences fully. Clearly Susan Hill offers comfort and reassurance to the victims of childhood's miseries by making them realise that their own experiences are not by any means unique and therefore that they themselves are not in any way marked out as different from other people. She is herself fully aware of this quality of her novel, and, though she obviously has not set out to write a *roman à thèse*, she is content that those who needed it have been able to find reassurance in her book.

Although her novel was inspired by her observation of two cheerful little boys during their summer holidays in the country, very little of this happiness has found its way into the novel. The view of childhood offered here is a dark, sombre picture of dull misery punctuated by sheer terror. This view contradicts the conventional picture of childhood, and again it has elicited a strong response from her young readers. Ironically, though she writes about children but not for children, her novel has been exceptionally successful with young people, and it might be said, perhaps, that it is a novel about childhood as experienced by children, not as remembered by adults.

Lack of love

I'm the King of the Castle is a chilling book: the dark and ugly house of Warings seems an appropriate background for the drama that is acted out there. The four people who are the cast of this drama all have one thing in common: there is no love in their lives, they have received none and have none to give. Edmund does not love his father, and, though he cries for his mother when he is asleep and suffering from a nightmare (Chapter 8), he does not seem to remember her with affection or miss her. Mr Hooper finds Edmund difficult and certainly unlovable. His concern for his son is largely an unease: he realises, though he shrinks from putting this into words even to himself, that the boy is not normal, and he is anxious that he himself should not be blamed for this: 'I shall not allow myself to feel guilty about it. Edmund will be like any other healthy boy. I am not to blame' (Chapter 4). His own childhood was without love, and so was his marriage, and though he is reluctant to admit it, the pattern is repeating itself in his relationship with his son.

It is doubtful whether he himself can love anyone: his feelings about Mrs Kingshaw are largely sexual, and he looks to her not for affection but for fulfilment of his erotic dreams. Yet he is not entirely without feelings: when Charles wakes from his nightmares after Edmund's accident and runs crying for his mother, Mr Hooper carries him downstairs to his mother and then back to bed, surely a gesture of kindness (Chapter 13).

Mrs Kingshaw shows concern for her son after Edmund's accident, but this instinctive emotion, which alarms Charles, seems to be lacking in affection: 'There was no warmth or comfort' (Chapter 13). At other times her tone is mostly one of irritation or of an artificial jollity, as she tries to give situations an acceptable conventional slant. If she loves her son truly, she is too preoccupied with her endless struggle for material security and respectability, for maintaining appearances while in constant financial difficulties, to spare much thought for him; and Charles, for all her nightly visits to his bedside, is as alone as if he were motherless. Having been given little affection he has none to give back to his mother, a fact of which she is undoubtedly aware. (She seems to have been hurt by his eagerness to part from her on his first arrival at boarding-school, when he was only seven years old, and though she praised him for being so brave, she wept a little over his cheerful letter home (Chapter 3).)

Anthony Fielding and his family are introduced by the author to provide a contrast to the four people at Warings. The affections are there, not shown in embarrassing public demonstrations, but given easily. Charles watches Fielding with his mother wistfully, aware that what he sees in the Fieldings' house is something he does not have himself: 'He thought, that is how you ought to be' (Chapter 14). It is implied that those who give and receive affection are given a security, an invulnerability not granted to those who have been deprived of love.

In her Afterword Susan Hill makes the curious remark 'But God help the trio of survivors.' It is curious for the light it sheds on the way a novelist works: it seems that the characters, once the author has given them life, have an existence independently of her, and will go on living after the events described in the novel have come to an end. Evidently she does not know (and must wonder, as we do) what will happen to these three people after Charles's death, but feels sure that their lives will be unhappy. With no real love for one another, will they go on living at

Warings? Will Mrs Kingshaw be able to persuade herself that in some unfathomable way Charles's death was an accident, and will the wedding go ahead? Will Edmund's father guess the full extent of Edmund's responsibility for Charles's death, and how will he cope with that knowledge? And, lastly, having exulted in Charles's death, will Edmund be able to resist exercising his cruelty on someone else? The French writer and philospher Jean Paul Sartre said that 'Hell is other people' (in his play *Huis Clos* (1944, *In Camera* in English), Scene V), and it seems certain that these three at least will find their loveless, bleak lives miserable enough to punish them for what they had done out of lack of love, lack of understanding, and, in Edmund's case, plain wickedness.

Isolation

The absence of love brings isolation. Language is an inadequate tool for expressing complex, indefinable emotions, and only love can bridge the gap between what one wants to say and what one can put into words. This is true of adults, and how can it be otherwise with children who do not possess the command of language and the verbal skill to formulate their thoughts in order to express their worst fears and deepest wishes?

There is a complete lack of communication between Edmund and his father, compounded of Mr Hooper's unconscious unwillingness to probe too deeply into his son's mind for fear of what he might find there, and of Edmund's secretiveness, his hardness, coldness, his reluctance to explain, to share his thoughts. Where the father is uneasy about their relationship, the son not only accepts the isolation, he desires it, feels at ease in it.

For different reasons there is no real communication between Charles and his mother either. To some extent this is the result of Mrs Kingshaw's way of thinking and speaking, her wish for a comfortable existence both material and emotional. She sees things as she wishes them to be, ignoring as much as possible anything that is unpleasant, inconveniently awkward. It is a measure of her complete misreading of the relationship between her son and Edmund that she refers to the latter as Charles's special friend. This absence of understanding makes it possible for Edmund's false accusations against Charles to be accepted by her as the truth, all the more easily because she is naturally aware of her own – and Charles's – subservient position in the house, and anxious not to be seen as favouring her own child.

As for Charles, he regards his mother as a potential embarrassment. She dresses too flashily, uses too much make-up for small boys' critical scrutiny, and Charles is much too young to judge her charitably, to understand her desperate desire to remarry, to have someone who would support her and allow her to give up thankfully the endless struggle for survival. He holds his mother at a distance so as not to be ashamed of her, and, having isolated himself from her and being unable to speak to her (an inability which most children share to some extent at least), he cannot explain to her how much his old school means to him, how terrible for him is the thought of joining Edmund at his school and being tormented by him there as well as at Warings.

In this way the characters' inability to communicate with one another, stemming from the absence of affection and trust, makes the tragedy of Charles's suicide understandable and indeed almost inevitable.

The power of evil

Surprisingly for a period of history that has known so much evil and cruelty, our age seems singularly reluctant to accept the existence of wickedness. Extenuating circumstances are offered in explanation, diminishing and trivialising what is an incontestable, frightening fact: that there are people who are simply bad, that evil exists and has great power. Susan Hill sees it as a demonic force taking possession of a young boy, and her conception of it seems also to indicate a belief that evil exists somehow outside the human heart, lying in wait to seize it by force. For her, evil is linked with the absence of love, which creates a vacuum for it to fill. In this way, if one is to believe in the existence of evil one must also believe in the power of love and in the negative power of lack of love. Folly, stupidity, lack of understanding are all born out of the absence of love, and it is the blindness of these defects that enables evil to take root and flourish.

There is no doubt, therefore, in Susan Hill's mind about the existence of evil: she believes in it as much as, and because, she believes in the power of love. Because there is no love in the novel (except for the fleeting warmth of the Fielding household), the power of evil is shown as great; and it triumphs. It is easy to dislike the novel because it does seem to picture evil as victorious, outraging our sense of the rightness of retribution – we want wickedness to be punished. It is possible that the novelist herself felt this need for assurance that somehow evil will not triumph in the end, and that it was for this reason that she included in her Afterword (written after an interval of eighteen years, during which time she had sufficient feedback from her readers to gauge the strength of their feelings) that sentence 'But God help the trio of survivors.' The power of evil is great, but retribution ultimately comes, is the message we receive.

Nature

The background of this novel is the southern English countryside, some-where not too far from the Downs; Susan Hill's love of the country is evident in her way of life and in the number of books she has published which celebrate the country. Yet in this novel nature appears not just indifferent but sometimes actively hostile. Early in the book, in Chapter 3, we read of the frightening incident with the monstrous crow that attacks Charles. Hang Wood and Barnard's Forest have a bad name in the village, and children do not dare to enter the wood. The woodshed in which Edmund locks Charles is full of nameless slimy things, and there might be rats and bats there. It seems that the novelist is determined to draw a parallel between this menacing world of nature and the behaviour of the people inside the house. Naturally on the Fieldings' farm there is cruelty: the calves will be sold to be slaughtered for veal, the turkeys will all be killed for Christmas, the birth of a calf is a painful, frightening business. The only difference is perhaps that on the farm the harsh actions are carried out in a matter-of-fact, speedy manner. The animals are killed for food, and the reason for the action is clearly understood.

In the end Charles makes the distinction between the impersonal menace of the woods, and the human menace of Edmund's deliberate cruelty, of Mr Hooper's blind insensitivity, of his own mother's uncaring incomprehension.

In the last days before his suicide Charles finds pleasure in watching the squirrels at play in the copse near the house, a family of wrens darting about an alder bush. On his way to kill himself he feels comforted and at ease in the wood, no longer afraid. Once before in Hang Wood he had felt happy, hidden away and safe, in his own phrase 'it was all quite all right' (Chapter 6). In his ultimate perception of the wood we might see a reconciliation between the dark image of Nature as cruel and menacing, which marks so much of the novel, and Susan Hill's own private delight in the countryside. The beauty is there, the feeling of being at peace in a place that delights the senses, and that, while it knows sudden pain and death, is safe from human cruelty and from evil, symbolised by the dark, ugly house of Warings.

Language and style

A marked characteristic of Susan Hill's writing is its plainness. The sentences are short, words are used sparingly, with great care. Where one adjective will suffice, only one will be used, and there are no lush descriptions, piling up the adjectives, striving to convey the picture in the writer's mind. As they are used so sparingly, of course, words have to carry their full weight of meaning. This seems to apply to verbs especially (feet crunch, or rustle and squeak, a mouse scuttles, birds dart and hop, leaves fidget) which are rarely amplified by adverbs.

One reason for the simplicity of style may be that though it never employs the first-person narrator, a large part of the novel relates the events as they are experienced by the boy Charles, and the style matches his quick-moving thoughts. This viewpoint accounts perhaps for some of the images, startlingly unexpected, extremely simple. Tree trunks are 'wrinkled and grey like the legs of elephants', with fungus which looks like 'pale suède' leather (Chapter 7); Charles's legs move like scissors when he is swimming (Chapter 9); the cow after calving is heavy like a camel (Chapter 14). These are not poetic images chosen as much for their sound and literary associations as for what they convey to the mind's eye, these images present objects which momentarily remind the boy of things he had seen.

As the imagery is simple, so are the thoughts and feelings, again conveyed through the sparing vocabulary of an eleven-year-old. It must be stressed though that the novelist makes no conscious, condescending effort to imitate a boy's manner of speaking (except perhaps in always referring to the boys by their surnames only, apparently following the private-school conventions). After all, the thoughts of Mr Hooper and Mrs Kingshaw are expressed in similarly brief sentences, nevertheless betraying something of each character's personality. Mrs Kingshaw, thinking of the planned excursion to Leydell Castle says to herself comfortably, 'it will be just as though we are one family' (Chapter 12), and on the morning of her wedding she thinks, 'this is the best thing that could have happened ... I shall not be a struggling, lonely woman now' (Chapter 17); while Mr Hooper, always weighed down by his sense of guilt, never quite admitting his own desires even to himself, thinks, 'Even though, when I advertised for a housekeeper, I had it in mind that ...', and he recollects that 'the way that she looked at him ... there was something ...' (Chapter 16).

The style of narrative is generally plain, and the author uses simple, neutral language that owes little to present-day fashions. However, there are contemporary references – the boys wear jeans, Charles in anger uses the famous four-letter word, the boys' conversation is sprinkled with expressions like 'dead clever', 'shut your face', 'stuff it!' Occurring amongst the neutral, simple language, these references may cause readers a shock of surprise, suddenly highlighting the fact that the novel has a contemporary setting. For the most part though, it is the plainness of the language that leaves the strongest impression, and may give the narrative its curious, timeless quality.

There is beauty in this simple language, especially in the descriptions of nature. As is to be expected in a writer who lives in the country and loves it, Susan Hill describes what she has undoubtedly often observed herself with delight: the reflection of the bright moon on a stream, hidden by trees and only observed when the wind moves the tree branches (Chapter 1), the hawthorn hedge 'draped with beaded cobwebs' (Chapter 5), the deer seen poised for flight, with its neck 'taut enough to snap' (Chapter 6), the wood lit up by lightning 'for a long, slow second' (Chapter 7).

As well as all these sharp, bright pictures of the countryside, there are other images in this novel which carry a deeper, symbolic meaning. There is the terrifying image of the crow: the monstrous crow which attacks Charles in the cornfield (Chapter 3), the stuffed crow which Edmund puts on Charles's bed (Chapter 3), the hooded crows in Charles's nightmare in the shed (Chapter 12) which comes back into his dreams after Edmund's accident (Chapter 13), the clown's open mouth like a crow's open beak (Chapter 16). All these are images of deathly malice, all the more powerful for their confused, nightmarish quality.

The second image of terror is the moths. Charles finds them physically repugnant and frightening, but their significance goes beyond the physical revulsion he feels. Like the Death's Head moth they are all symbols of death, of the negation of life, and it is characteristic of the Hooper family that their family heirloom should have been a collection of dead moths, further reminding us of death, and that old Mr Hooper on his deathbed should have resembled a white moth.

Hang Wood, too, has a meaning over and above the physical. Dark and menacing at first, sinister like its name, the wood changes for Charles, becoming a place of safety, a hiding-place from torment. He cannot run away from Edmund even in the wood, but at least there he feels himself for a time to be superior to him: he is not frightened of thunder, he finds the clearing with the stream, he catches a fish, he drags Edmund up from the bank and revives him, makes a fire and a hot drink, stops Edmund's hysterical screaming. All these actions take place in the wood and give Charles self-confidence, if only temporarily.

Similarly, although Charles is afraid of the openness of the castle ruins, they give him his moment of triumph when he is the King of the Castle, exulting over his enemy – though again only briefly. Like the wood then, the castle is something of an ambiguous symbol, embodying danger as well as the assurance of a personal achievement.

Finally, there is Warings, the Hoopers' Victorian house, bleak and ugly with yew trees and rhododendrons pressing round it. To the Hoopers, both father and son, it is a symbol of family pride, of inherited possessions, but to Charles it is threatening, evil, with dark watching windows, a terrible house with its stuffed animals and boxes of dead moths – a house of death, with death, paradoxically, the only means of escape from it. (It is revealing that Mr Hooper, though proud of the house, is evidently uneasy about it. Surely both his proposals for improving the house, redecorating it and clearing out the attics have some symbolic meaning of renewal, of casting off the past.)

Thus things described in plain, simple words possess a deeper meaning; and the reader comes to share Charles's terror as he runs helplessly this way and that, finding no way out. These symbols of cruelty and death are truly terrible in their ordinariness, and the plain writing serves to heighten the effect, leaving it to the reader's imagination to depict them fully.

Characters

I'm the King of the Castle takes its title from a nursery rhyme which presents the rivalry between two children ('I'm the king of the castle, and you're a dirty rascal'). The theme of the novel, too, is the struggle between two boys (and, ultimately, between good and evil), and the characters of the two protagonists in this struggle matter very much. Though the boys do have a short, silent fight early in their relationship (Chapter 2), the struggle between them is largely non-physical, a psychological campaign of terror waged by Edmund against Charles in which of course the victim's nature dictates the methods used to break him. Charles's character therefore shapes the whole book.

Charles Kingshaw

By the end of the novel the reader will have gathered a great deal of information about Charles. As was mentioned above, in the section on 'Structure and technique', much of the action is seen through his eyes, and in addition we learn a lot about him from his fragmented recollections of his past life.

He is of average intelligence, not outstandingly bright, and fully aware of this: 'He had never been much good at anything . . . He was the sort of boy whose name people forgot' (Chapter 5); 'he was only good at plodding along by himself, not at competing' (Chapter 15). He is not physically brave, not like a boy at his school, Fenwick, whom he admired for his ability to bear pain (Chapter 14).

He is aware, however, of his own inner strength, of his capacity for endurance, which has been tested often, and he knows that this capacity is something his enemy lacks. Yet this knowledge is of no use to him in the struggle with Edmund: Charles is a born victim, symbolically singled out for a senseless attack by the crow in Chapter 3, as he had been singled out at school by Lesage, the Deputy Senior Prefect, possibly for hidden sexual reasons (Chapter 13).

At school the only thing at which he really excelled was climbing. He was the only boy to have reached the crow's nest at the top of the elm tree by the South Gate (Chapter 12).

These are qualities of which he is aware in himself. Another quality which he possesses – without realising it – is his ability to see himself clearly and dispassionately, accepting his own weaknesses, and we can only speculate about the loneliness of his childhood which has fostered the habit of introspection.

Charles is also able to see his relationships with other people clearly: he is aware of the weight of his mother's ambitions for him and of his own inability to fulfil them, to win the scholarships which would enable him to get on in life. Again, he is quite clear about what makes his friendship with Anthony Fielding so special, that it is something of his own, unspoiled by Edmund's malice. When his mother blunders in inviting Fielding to tea, Charles feels that his friendship is now finished, ruined: 'I've finished with you, I'd rather be just me, me, me' (Chapter 16).

Though he is not physically brave, he has courage born of desperation and fortitude, as he shows when he stops himself from screaming when he sees the stuffed crow on his bed (Chapter 3). For such a young boy he has remarkable forethought, and lays his plans for running away efficiently (though it was a mistake not to take any water with him, this was not because he forgot but because he was worried about the extra weight to carry). He is quite good with his hands, too: his helter-skelter model of which he is so proud works very well, and he seems to have the practical ability to plan his models in advance, working them out carefully on graph paper.

His moral instincts are sound: he is worried about taking food with him when he runs away, and can only reassure himself by the reflection that he would have been eating the food if he stayed in the house, and that therefore he is not guilty of stealing. He does not abandon Edmund in the forest, though he hates and fears him, because he knows that he cannot bring himself to do such a thing (Chapter 7), and similarly, standing high on the wall of the castle, he will not push Edmund off the ledge and kill him, even though he does wish him dead: 'He knew that he would not' (Chapter 12). These are true moral decisions, and he makes them because he knows that he could not bear the guilt for his actions if he gave in to temptation.

He has a tender heart towards animals, perhaps channelling to them his affectionate instincts for which he has no outlet elsewhere. The crow frightens him and he is repelled by moths, but he deeply regrets letting the fish he has caught die painfully on dry land (Chapter 8) and he cannot bring himself to kill the rabbit he has caught (Chapter 7). Most tellingly he finds the circus unbearable because of the tasselled caps the elephants are made to wear and because of 'the docile expression in their eyes'. He is aware of the humiliation of the trained wild animals and of their pain (Chapter 16). The fate of farm animals, destined for slaughter, makes him want to cry, as he imagines their terror (Chapter 14).

When Edmund is hysterical with fear in the forest, and later, when he is ill and frightened in the night, Charles speaks kindly to him, even though he knows that as soon as the situation returns to normal Edmund will start bullying him again, and he will be unable to use his knowledge of Edmund's breakdown and fear successfully against him. This seems to be the key to his character, his awareness of other people, and therefore of their weaknesses, and his inability to exploit this knowledge because of the strength of his own moral instincts.

Also, though he has a very adult-like perception of himself and of

Edmund, he is a child still, and has no way of putting into words convincingly what he knows to be the truth: Edmund's lies, his treachery, his cruelty. Charles's simple code prevents him from calling out when he has been locked up in the Red Room and again in the shed, and of accusing Edmund of these wrongs. When he speaks out, as after the incident with the helter-skelter model, he can only shout incoherently in his rage, inviting the adults' disapproval and punishment.

He seems never to have received much affection or understanding, even when his father was alive and, presumably, his family life was stable. His father laughed at his childish fears of the booming vastness of the indoor swimming-pool and of the distorted bodies of the swimmers. Whatever affection his mother has for him, she has no instinctive understanding of her son, belittles his dread of the circus and ignores his physical distress there. Most important of all, she totally misreads the relationship between the two boys and seems blithely ignorant of her son's misery. Charles's emotional isolation and the lack of any real understanding between him and his mother make him an easy target for Edmund's bullying.

Charles is aware of the absence of a loving relationship with his mother. Starved of real affection, he enjoys the security of Mr Hooper's arms round him even while he is ashamed of his need. (There are very similar characters in some of Susan Hill's other novels. The boy James Fount in *A Change for the Better* (1976) is similarly burdened by his mother's expectations of him and deprived of any real affection, while John Hilliard, the young officer of the First World War in her novel *Strange Meeting* (1973) is what Charles might have grown into if he had lived – solitary, uncommunicative, incapable of love until he meets David Barton and makes the acquaintance of David's large, cheerful, loving family.)

Charles has made himself independent of his mother quite deliberately: 'he never did go to her, he made himself cope alone' (Chapter 3). Lack of love has made him turn in towards himself, away from people because they cannot be trusted. His fear of being hurt makes him vulnerable; he knows this, and knows also that from the moment they met, Edmund knew that he would always be able to terrorise him. Watching Edmund trying to frighten Fielding and retreating, baffled by Fielding's cheerful indifference, Charles feels the cruel injustice of his own predicament. The same stoic endurance that has stood him in good stead at other times makes him accept the inevitability of his fate now: Edmund will always be there, Edmund will always know how to torment him, there is no escape other than through the pool in the clearing.

Having been able to accept the miseries of his wanderings with his mother, the humiliations of a socially and financially insecure existence have prepared him to accept as necessary and right the act of killing himself. Tragically, most of his short life has been a painful preparation for suicide.

Edmund Hooper

Unlike the character of Charles, that of Edmund is never clearly delineated. To a considerable degree this is due, of course, to the events of the novel being observed through Charles's eyes. While his motives and emotions are described and explained, we remain in the dark about Edmund.

We know that he is about the same age as Charles but looks younger and is more immature in some ways; he is 'breathing heavily onto the paper, like a much smaller child' when colouring (Chapter 2). His face is expressionless, and he is pale, presumably because he does not much like leaving the house. His favourite occupations are sedentary, making plasticine models or compiling lists of regiments and drawing maps of battles (there may be some significance in his liking for war and battles which offends his father). He offers scornful criticism of Charles's model, but it seems doubtful whether he has the manual skill to make anything himself, and he certainly is less able to look after himself in the wood than Charles.

We know nothing about his life at school. He tells Charles that he will be Head of Dorm and that he can order the other boys in the dormitory to maltreat Charles. He boasts of the many friends he has at school, but we may remember that while Charles had been invited by two school friends to spend the holidays with them and has received postcards from them, there has been no mention of Edmund's friends writing to contact him.

He is a watcher, someone who remains on the outside. His is the face at the window, looking out. It seems clear that the persecution of Charles becomes an obsession with him, a totally absorbing game. He collects information about his enemy, from the loquacious Mrs Kingshaw, from listening and watching, and certainly from being able to enter Charles's mind.

Where Charles reacts with understandable rage when he finds that his precious helter-skelter model has been given to Edmund, Edmund's own reaction to the destruction of his battle plans and lists of regiments is quite different. He waits, knowing that his silence will frighten and worry Charles, and then, typically during the night and unseen, he pushes his sinister message under Charles's door. His reaction is revealing in two ways: it shows his understanding of Charles's psychology and his unnatural restraint, particularly strange in a child.

Like many children from private schools Edmund is a dreadful snob, and finds his father's superior position as Mrs Kingshaw's employer a useful weapon against Charles. He likes Warings and its contents, sharing his father's family pride, but again his family possessions are to him another means of humiliating Charles.

He seems to have an instinctive knowledge of Charles's weaknesses. Even when they are lost in the wood and preparing unhappily to spend the night there, Edmund finds the opportunity to play on Charles's fear of moths, telling him that there will be moths in the wood, 'Pretty big ones, as well' (Chapter 7). He guesses at once at Charles's misery in the circus too.

Quite early in their relationship Edmund realises suddenly that it gives him exquisite pleasure to think of things to do to Charles, to hurt him (Chapter 3). Like a skilled torturer he knows where to hurt. Yet he has his own soft spots too. He is hysterical with fear in the thunderstorm, and again at the moment of their realisation that they are lost in the wood. In the night he has a nightmare and screams for his mother (which, incidentally, surprises Charles). Yet his weaknesses seem irrelevant, as Charles is incapable of exploiting them, and so, once Edmund's hysterical fits have passed, the relationship remains the same. Have there been other victims before Charles, at school? We may well wonder.

It seems certain that there has been no affection in his own life. His mother, who was apparently the only person capable of dealing with him, is dead, and, though he calls for her in his sleep, apparently he does not miss her in his waking hours. (Though we may wonder at his vicious mockery of Mrs Kingshaw's good-night visits to her son's bedroom – how much jealousy is there behind the spite?)

Edmund's relationship with his father is quite without affection on both sides. Edmund despises his father and pays no attention to him, while Mr Hooper is clearly uneasy about his son. He sees in the boy his wife, for whom he had had no love or liking, and he evidently suspects that the boy is not normal. Though he can hardly have made out his son's real nature he knows enough about him to feel guilty. As any parent would, he feels that whatever is wrong with the boy is his own fault (though he also blames his wife for dying and leaving him no set of rules to follow in bringing up the child), and is all the more desperately anxious to see the child as normal.

Edmund's emotional isolation appears to be total, though we must remember that, as has been said above in the section on 'Structure and technique', we are rarely allowed to share his thoughts, and know almost nothing of his life before the beginning of the story.

He is intelligent, probably brighter than Charles, and in some ways more worldly than his enemy: he is the first to guess the growing attraction between his father and Charles's mother, and he surmises accurately enough that Mrs Kingshaw would like to marry again. Yet he is a child too; we may remember his habit of raising his eyebrows because he has seen one of his teachers do this, and naïvely thinks of it as 'an impressive way of looking' (Chapter 2). On one occasion, and one occasion only, does Edmund really act like a child: when he and Charles play at hunters in the forest. The incident is all the more remarkable for being an isolated instance, out of character, out of place. At all other times Edmund is engaged in his solitary pursuits or in his persecution of Charles.

The hatred, which is reciprocated, is sudden: it starts as a resentment of intruders but almost at once it turns into an obsessive dislike. The remarkable thing is, of course, that because we are granted hardly any insights into Edmund's mind, we tend only to see the outward manifestations of his hatred – the persecution, the bullying, the tormenting; we are shown no reasons for them. Where Charles articulates his dislike of Edmund, at least to himself, Edmund acts in silence, keeping his thoughts to himself, and the reader is seldom privy to them.

The hatred seems irrational in its intensity, a motiveless self-indulgence in cruelty which can only be described as evil. Here we return to what is the central trait of Edmund's character, and perhaps the reason why the processes of his mind are kept secret from us. He is, in the end, lacking in humanity, simply evil, and as evil is incomprehensible and irrational, the motives of the actions of this child, whether he is possessed by evil as an outside power, or was born wicked, must remain hidden. The rationale for his behaviour, the mystery of evil, makes Edmund's character impossible for us to understand and indeed hard to envisage.

Mr Joseph Hooper

Although Mr Hooper is one of the two secondary characters, the reader learns quite a lot about him in the course of the novel. He had an unhappy childhood, presumably because his parents were strict and unloving, and he remembers the misery of his young days well, though he will try to pretend to himself that he was happy as a child. Evidently he was not an only child, but his sisters, 'the girls', do not seem to figure in his adult life. He was not allowed to play outside much; instead he had to sit and watch his father working on his collections in the Red Room. Too frightened of his father to do otherwise, he pretended to be interested in his father's work while loathing the whole business. Later, when he was older, he rebelled, and quarrelled bitterly with his father. He only returned to the house after his mother's death, when his father lay unconscious, dying.

Old Mr Hooper was a man of character and ability, a good businessman as well as a renowned lepidopterist, who despised his son. Mr Hooper knows in his heart that his father was right to treat him with contempt. He knows that by comparison with his father he himself has achieved nothing, that he has no striking qualities. Tall, thin and grey, with eyes the colour of seaweed, he knows that he does not cut an impressive figure. His marriage was unhappy; his wife found his sexual demands tiresome and treated him coldly, thus adding to his low estimation of himself.

There certainly is nothing loving about his relationship with his son. Mr Hooper sees a strong likeness between his son and his late wife, not only in appearance but also in the boy's cold, self-contained, secretive nature. He knows that the boy is not quite normal, though he does not seem to be able or willing to define the quality that sets his son apart from other boys. He is aware nevertheless that there is something wrong with the boy, as is shown by his constant feelings of guilt about him.

We may wonder to what extent Mr Hooper's fears about his son contribute to Charles's hopeless predicament. If Mr Hooper is unwilling to face the truth about Edmund he will be equally unwilling to accept that it is Edmund who persecutes Charles, that Edmund should be punished while Charles should be protected from his son's malice.

In some ways Mr Hooper appears to be afraid of Edmund; he does not dare to hit him, much as he would like to, when the boy is insolent, while he has no hesitation about striking Charles who is shouting his protest when his helter-skelter was given to Edmund without his consent. (In this painful scene, which demonstrates the adults' total lack of understanding of the true nature of the boys' relationship, Mr Hooper may be repeating the pattern of his own childhood when he was beaten by his stern father.)

It is significant that Mr Hooper looks to Mrs Kingshaw to be a willing partner in acting out his erotic dreams. Evidently he does not seek affection in his marriage, presumably because he neither needs nor is capable of giving love.

He is hoping that his miserable existence in the large, gloomy house will take a turn for the better with the arrival of Mrs Kingshaw. He plans to have the house redecorated; to clear out the lumber in the attics; he gives a Sunday morning cocktail party to widen his circle of friends; and from the very beginning of his acquaintance with Mrs Kingshaw he has marriage in mind. Her fluttering admiration boosts his self-confidence, and he takes the initiative in planning family outings, and, more significantly, transferring Charles to Edmund's school. In financial terms this is a generous action, presumably inspired by a laudable resolution to treat both boys equally after his marriage to Charles's mother. Although uneasy about his son's character, he clearly does not fully realise just how abnormal Edmund is, and what effect his relentless persecution has on Charles. Stupidity of this kind is unpardonable, and there is no doubt that to deprive Charles of any relief from Edmund's bullying is to drive him to take that last, desperate action.

Clearly Mr Hooper neither understands Charles's desperation nor has any real desire to do so, as he would then have to face the reality of his own son's character. It is characteristic of his disregard of the boy that during their taxi ride in London he continues to point out London landmarks when the boy has told him that he used to live in London. Mr Hooper does not listen because he does not care, in this trivial incident as well as in the important decisions he takes it upon himself to make for the boy. Through him, and through Mrs Kingshaw, Susan Hill stresses the impact of crass insensibility and blind disregard of others which can have an effect just as devastating as deliberate cruelty.

Mrs Helena Kingshaw

Charles's mother may be seen by many readers as a pathetic figure, deserving our pity. She struggles hard to support herself and her son through a series of jobs which indicate clearly that she has no qualifications, apart from having run a home while her husband was alive. The jobs are poorly paid, unsatisfactory, and never seem to last for very long. Not surprisingly, Charles comes to see his school as his home, an attitude which is understandable, but which effectively excludes his mother and contributes to the absence of any real affection between them.

Charles is more than a little ashamed of his mother. The boys at school make fun of him because his mother uses too much make-up and dresses flashily. He looks wistfully at Mrs Fielding, the working farmer's wife, who wears trousers, whose hair is straight, who smiles briefly and says little, and whose relationship with her son seems so easy and natural. We may realise here that Charles and his mother never seem to talk to one another or enjoy each other's company. Mrs Kingshaw is not comfortable with her son, and worries whether she is a good mother to him, whether she says the right things to him and looks at ease in his presence (Chapter 5).

Naturally enough for a woman accustomed to dependence on her husband, Mrs Kingshaw hopes to marry again. She is lonely, frightened of the future, and misses the comfort of the physical relationship with her husband. There is some truth, it seems, in Edmund's sneering enquiry as to whether Mrs Kingshaw had 'gone after a lot of people' (Chapter 8). It is no wonder then that she is determined to succeed at Warings, flattering Mr Hooper, trying to ingratiate herself with both father and son. Again external circumstances contribute to Charles's desperate isolation. His mother does not really know much about him, and does not even notice, let alone consider seriously, the misery of his existence under Edmund's rule of terror. Uncertain of her position in the house and anxious to please and attract Mr Hooper, she is unlikely to question any accusation hurled by Edmund at her son. Though she remarks on the change in Charles's behaviour, it does not seem to occur to her to examine this change, to check whether the facts of each incident are as Edmund claims, and indeed to wonder why her son should act so out of character. While Charles is aware of the change in himself, thinking, 'The way he was behaving was entirely new to him' (Chapter 10), he is also conscious of the change in his mother, of a 'new sharpness and impatience' in her (Chapter 15), and he feels that she is behaving to him in this way to please Mr Hooper.

Mrs Kingshaw is neither very intelligent nor perceptive and she has a conventional and shallow mind. To every crisis she responds with a comfortable cliché and a hot drink, and it is unlikely that she could bring herself to accept the reality of Edmund's cruelty. It is her habit to ignore or minimise anything socially awkward or unpleasant: talking of Charles's dread of circuses she says that he 'used to be a little bit frightened. But of course all that is quite forgotten, and this is going to be a simply splendid treat' (Chapter 16). To Edmund, seeing her son's body floating in the pool she says pathetically, 'you mustn't look and be upset, everything is all right'. The irony of these words will not be lost on the reader: Edmund has looked and seen, and triumphed; he will not be upset because he has no human feelings which could be disturbed by the sight, and nothing will be all right, because it is her son who has drowned himself. For once her comforting clichés are no longer comic or even irritating, they are profoundly wrong and shocking, summing up her part in the tragedy.

Like Mr Hooper, but for different reasons, she has been deliberately blind and stupid, and though, given the nature of her relationship with Charles and her circumstances, it would have been unrealistic to expect her to see the truth of the situation and do something about it, she bears her share of the guilt. She betrayed her son, giving no real thought to his happiness, and though she might be able to create her own more comfortable version of the tragedy, enough doubt will surely remain in her mind as she looks back, to make any real happiness impossible, for how could she go on living at Warings (that is, supposing that the marriage will still take place), seeing Edmund daily, and wondering about his relationship with her son? Speculating, as readers often do when they have finished reading a novel, about the future life of the leading characters, we may remember the author's remark in the Afterword, 'But God help the trio of survivors.' For Mrs Kingshaw the punishment would be to have to face the facts of the case and her part in events, stripped of comfortable euphemisms, and to know that she too helped through her selfishness and lack of understanding to bring about her boy's death.

Anthony Fielding

Though his part in the plot is a small one, Anthony Fielding plays a significant role in the novel. His cheerful normality is a yardstick against which the other characters can be measured, and helps to stress the appalling situation at Warings. He has a small, deeply tanned face, which makes him look old, and he has long eyelashes which look to Charles like spiders' legs. That is all we know of his physical appearance, as observed by Charles.

He is a cheerful, happy boy, outgoing, on friendly terms with everyone in the village of Derne, yet he is no callous extrovert. He seems to guess at Charles's feelings without being able to understand them, and he is kind and protective towards his new friend. When he and Charles play and talk, we are witnessing the only cheerful, honest, friendly conversation between two people who are at ease with each other and enjoying themselves, in the whole novel.

He seems to be the only person who has the ability to deal with Edmund, treating him with cheerful indifference, and showing unconsciously that he is not afraid of him, though he finds him odd and a little boring.

His other function is to stress Charles's isolation once their friendship has been spoiled by Mrs Kingshaw's crass interference. Charles retreats into himself, free of all human ties now, safe in his loneliness, going to the pool in the clearing with no regrets. He has had a taste of uncomplicated happiness just to make him realise that this is not for him. With Fielding gone all humanity goes out of the story.

Part 4

Hints for study

Reading the text

Your first reading of the chosen work should be for pleasure. You will need to analyse the novel at a later stage, to read it with a view to studying its structure, identifying the main themes, examining the language and imagery, but your first reading is not likely to allow you to dissect the novel, especially if you are mainly interested in the story.

When you have finished your first reading spare a little time to think about it. By now you will have some idea of what kind of novel you are studying, what you particularly like or dislike about it, and which aspects of it are in your opinion likely to be the subject of coursework or examination questions. Note down these first impressions; you may find them useful later. Indeed you may find that some of your best ideas came to you during this first reading, though you may not yet have fully formulated them at this stage.

Now comes the second reading. This time you will be considering the novel as a literary work, as distinct from an interesting story. You should be making notes as you read, perhaps under headings such as those used in the Commentary above (though you may wish to substitute headings of your own if you have decided on a line you will take in your discussion of the novel). You will find it useful to consider the structure of the novel, the shaping of it, the way it is laid out. See if you can identify the key incidents essential to the development of the plot. Try to jot down the story in the briefest possible form, and then see how the author went about the telling of it, giving the novel its distinctive character.

What about the use of dialogue, and of flashback? Identify the narrator: is it the author's voice, speaking impartially, or does she allow the characters to speak for themselves, and if so, how?

So far you have been thinking about the novelist's technique of presenting the story. Now give some thought to what she wanted to tell you apart from the story, what were the ideas that inspired her novel and made it into the dark tale it is. The author has made this part of your work easy for you, stating as she does in the Afterword what her novel is about – children, cruelty, evil, lack of love, isolation. You may think of other themes that have struck you – say, the relations between parents and children, the inability to communicate, the role of nature in the novel. List the themes and try to remember incidents which illustrate them. Make a note of them, remembering to write down page numbers as well, as you will want to verify later that such incidents are relevant to your argument.

If a novel's structure and technique are concerned with the way the plot unfolds, and themes with the ideas that inspired the book, the way the story is told is the novel's style, the language the author uses. You should make careful notes on the style during your second reading. By this time you will be familiar with the story, and able to concentrate on the form. Remember to note down the page references for any passages that strike you, whether for the images used or for the way a passage shapes your view of a character. Mark any passages that you might like to learn by heart; better to try to memorise phrases short enough for you to quote accurately later.

Go through the novel and think of the use of language. Does the novelist employ recurring images, symbolising the themes (for instance, the crow as a symbol of evil and cruelty)? Susan Hill's language is simple, but is it effective? Does it reflect the characters concerned, does it change with a different character's viewpoint? Are the dialogues convincing; do the people speak like people you know? What about the descriptions? You might select a few passages which seem to you the most characteristic, and either learn them by heart, or write down brief summaries of them, identifying them clearly (for instance, 'Charles's dream of the puppet theatre, the appearance of the hooded crows' in Chapter 11).

Now is the time to organise your material. List your comments under the various headings, supporting your views with examples from the text, always with page numbers, as you may need to check the appropriateness of your illustrations later. Go over your notes slowly, considering your material for its usefulness in answering questions on the novel. You may find that your notes already give you an idea or two for possible essays, which you might like to sketch out as good examination practice. (You will also find a list of specimen questions – with specimen answers – below, page 53).

Preparing for an examination

Having tried your hand at one or two examination questions, you should test yourself by writing an essay under examination conditions. First you must check how much time you will have in the examination, and how many questions you will be expected to answer. Work out the time available for each question, allowing extra time, first for reading through the paper with care and deciding which questions you will answer, and, second, for reading through your answers at the end, to correct any spelling errors that might have crept in, and to supply any words which you might have missed out.

Now start timing your answer. First work out roughly what you want to say, and make a plan: a brief introduction, the main part setting out your views, and a closing section as a summing-up. Check your rough plan against the question, to make sure that you are answering it, and keeping to the point of the question. (It is a good idea to keep on glancing at the wording of the question as you write: you will lose marks if you stray from the point.) Include any quotations you have prepared but only if they are relevant; do not try to drag them in just because you spent time learning them. If you are not absolutely sure of the exact wording, do not attempt to quote; paraphrase instead.

When you have finished, go over your answer carefully, correcting any errors. If you find you have not got the time to finish your answer, write a brief note, such as you would write for the examiner, showing the line your reasoning was going to take: here your rough plan may be of use.

Such practice is useful. There is a difference, of course, between practising at home and writing in an examination room, under stress, pressed for time; but the virtue of practice in essay writing is that it will make your task in the examination a little less unfamiliar, and therefore easier to deal with. Having written a few answers at home, all dealing with different aspects of the novel, you will have acquired the knack of organising your thoughts in required form and length. (Always remember that it is *your* thoughts that the examiner wants to learn about: do not be afraid to disagree with the statement in a question, as long as you can support your views by references to the text.)

Specimen questions

(1) Discuss the theme of lovelessness in the novel.

(2) In her Afterword Susan Hill condemns Edmund Hooper: does her treatment of him in the novel support this condemnation?

(3) Choose an incident in the novel and describe it through Edmund's eyes.

(4) 'But God help the trio of survivors' – discuss this statement.

(5) The events in Hang Wood take up about a quarter of the book: do you think these events play an essential role in the novel?

(6) What is the significance of Anthony Fielding in the novel?

(7) Discuss the use of flashbacks in the novel.

(8) Draw a comparison between the children in *I'm the King of the Castle* and the boys in William Golding's *The Lord of the Flies* (or another book about children).

(9) Which incidents in the book would you describe as indispensable to the plot? Give your reasons.

(10) Why do you think this novel is so popular with young readers, and disliked by many adults?

(11) Discuss Susan Hill's treatment of nature.

Specimen answers

(4) 'But God help the trio of survivors' – discuss this statement.

These words from Susan Hill's Afterword to the novel are interesting on two counts.

First, they illustrate a phenomenon which has been described by a number of novelists, namely that the characters which they have created seem to them to acquire a life of their own, and become quite independent of their creators.

Many novelists see themselves almost as instruments of an outside creative force, with no control over the actions of the creatures of their imagination. It might of course be argued that if the novelist has achieved his or her purpose and created convincingly human characters, then it is to be expected that they will act in a manner consistent with the mental and emotional make-up given to them by the author. Yet the implication of Susan Hill's words amounts to something more than that. She seems to mean that to her the characters do not just behave in a way over which she feels that she has no control; they will go on living beyond the limits of her novel, and all she can do is to wonder what will happen to them. It should perhaps be added here, in parentheses, that not all novelists share her view of the writer's role. W. M. Thackeray, for example, makes semi-contemptuous reference to the main characters in his *Vanity Fair* as puppets to be tidied away in a box once the play is over.

Second, her words may also be read as an expression of a belief in the retribution that will be suffered at some future date by the three survivors of the tragedy in her novel. The book ends with Charles's death and Edmund's triumph, all the more intolerable because his role in the tragedy has gone undetected: his lies have been taken for truth and Charles's mother is actually trying to shield him from seeing the body of his victim. In the novel, then, good does not triumph and evil goes unpunished. It seems that the author herself, like her readers, finds it unacceptable that this should be so, and, speaking for us all (and, like us, ignorant of what will happen to them beyond the confines of the novel), she feels that the three people responsible for Charles's death must be found out by some divine justice, and that they will certainly live miserable lives.

A nineteenth-century novelist would have ended the book with a reassuring summary, however brief, showing how all three got their just deserts, nicely proportioned according to the degree of their guilt. Such neat tidying-up of loose ends is no longer acceptable in fiction today, and so we find the author satisfying her own, and her readers', desire for some sort of justice, by this one brief sentence in her Afterword.

It is a matter of taste whether the readers are satisfied with an indirect hint at the misery that lies ahead for the three guilty survivors, or whether they would prefer a more detailed report of their fate. The main point is that this one short sentence in the Afterword testifies to the readers' hunger for reassurance that this is, after all, a just world. And the tacit acknowledgement of this need is just as interesting as the glimpse into the writer's workshop which this one sentence also offers.

---

(7) Discuss the use of flashbacks in the novel.

The flashback is a well-established device of the modern novel. Recollections of the past had of course been used by novelists before our time, but the flashback, true to its name and its associations with the cinema, has a distinctive character of its own. It is a brief glimpse of the past, introduced abruptly and without explanation, clarifying or amplifying the present.

In *I'm the King of the Castle* we find a number of flashbacks, almost all of them telling us about Charles's life at school and in the private hotel where he and his mother lived for some time. They are very revealing: he was happy at school because he felt safe there, having learnt how to cope with the masters and the other boys. We realise also that, unusually, he was not homesick, because his home was not a warm, affectionate one, and there was no real understanding between himself and his mother. The flashbacks also reveal a lot about Charles's character, about the way he understands his own limitations, about his anxiety to do the right thing, and about his private terrors which tell us about his vivid imagination and sensitivity.

We also gain some insight into Mr Hooper's past life, his loveless childhood and later his loveless marriage, his sexual desires, his self-doubts and his guilt about Edmund. These insights explain the attraction Mrs Kingshaw has for him, and his lack of understanding of Charles's nature and his problems: a man whose childhood was miserable, who had been oppressed by a harsh father, may not be able to see into the mind of a boy whose life might seem easy to him by comparison.

When we consider the remaining two of the quartet of protagonists, we realise that we have been told virtually nothing about their past. Mrs Kingshaw seems to be making a deliberate effort not to think about the past at all, presumably because she has had to struggle too hard to keep herself and Charles, and she is determined to make a success of her relationship with Mr Hooper. She has probably had marriage in mind from the beginning, quite as much as Mr Hooper. Any absence of revealing glimpses of her past is probably a reflection of her attitude to life, no more.

When we come to Edmund, however, the omission is significant, especially in contrast to Charles. On reflection we realise that except for Edmund's recollection of his visit to his grandfather's deathbed and a brief reference to his mother, we know nothing of what his life has been like, nothing about his school (except for his boast about the many friends he has there, which sounds quite unconvincing). Indeed we rarely know what he is thinking, and the motives of his singularly mean and cruel actions remain hidden. Presumably this has been the author's intention throughout – to keep his thoughts dark, to tell us nothing about his past, and let us see the cruelty and evil malice of his mind all the more clearly because it is viewed in isolation. In such treatment of his character there is no room for the flashback which would help the reader to understand, to some extent at least, such apparently motiveless malice.

What began as a solitary child's understandable resentment of intruders, especially of one of his own age, a potential rival, develops into an obsessive desire to torment, and Edmund finds a lot of pleasure in satisfying it. In a rare insight into his mind the author tells us that this pleasure surprises Edmund: 'He could not have imagined the charm it afforded him, having Kingshaw here, thinking of things to do to him' (Chapter 3).

From his father's unease we may guess that there have been perhaps other indications, other incidents pointing to the potential for evil in Edmund's mind, but all we have is hints and surmises, not facts or certainties. The flashback, which could have helped us to understand, is deliberately not used, so as to keep the boy's character and motives a mystery.

By its very absence, then, the flashback remains a significant factor in establishing Edmund's character. Whereas our knowledge of Charles's past thoughts enables us to understand the actions that he takes, and sympathise with them, our lack of knowledge about Edmund ensures that he remains strange and alien to us, and we are therefore unable to form a sympathetic bond with him.

---

(11) Discuss Susan Hill's treatment of nature.

When it comes to the treatment of nature one might almost say that two authors were at work in this novel. For one, nature is a symbol of all that is cruel and evil in the book. The crow which attacks Charles turns into a nightmarish symbol of evil in the form of the stuffed bird on his bed, and insinuates itself into his worst dreams. The moths, both the dead ones in old Mr Hooper's collections, and the live ones, fluttering silently and blindly, terrify Charles. His terror is partly a personal, purely physical revulsion at touching their furry bodies and dry, dusty wings, and partly a horror of what the moths come to mean to him. Like the Death's Head moth, they are all symbols of night, of death. Charles may be only dimly aware of the symbolism, but his terror is very real.

Nature in the novel can be cruel and so can man. The thrush kills the snail (the whole process watched intently by Edmund), and the farmer rears calves and turkeys for slaughter. The dead rabbit, at first an object of pity, turns into a maggoty horror, a reminder of the reality of death.

Charles sees pain and terror everywhere. Hang Wood itself can be a menacing presence, waiting to capture and destroy.

There is, however, another side to Susan Hill's view of nature, no longer a symbol of terror, but a joy to see, bringing peace of mind. Even Hang Wood, which can engulf and stifle, also protects and shelters, becoming a place of safety from the storm: 'It was all right', as Charles says. The call of the deer in the wood is frightening to the boys at first, but when seen the animal is beautiful. As soon as Charles enters Hang Wood on the last day of his life, he grows calm, sure, almost happy; he knows now that he is doing the right thing. It might be said that the wood comes to represent the seductive side of death as a peaceful haven.

The positive power of the beauty of nature is emphasised at other points in the novel. Charles is able to forget his persecution briefly and take comfort when watching the squirrels at play or the family of wrens darting about. At such moments the trees and the woodland animals are no longer symbols of the human predicament; they are simply themselves, and to watch them is to put aside one's fears and simply be. These are moments of quiet delight, such as we feel the author, who lists country walking among her hobbies in *Who's Who*, might have experienced herself.

Such peaceful moments are rare in this novel, however. The novelist uses them as quiet interludes in her tale of terror, and uses them sparingly. Their function is to emphasise her dark story by contrast, as a distant, faint reminder of the happiness that has no place here. Here people inflict pain on one another and the world of nature reflects uncaringly the cruelty and indifference of man to man.

Part 5

Suggestions for further reading

The text

HILL, SUSAN: *I'm the King of the Castle*, Penguin Books, Harmondsworth, 1974, repr. with an Afterword 1988, 1989; Longman Imprint Books, Harlow, 1981.

Both of these are paperback editions, and there is no hardback edition available at present.

Other books by Susan Hill

HILL, SUSAN: *Air and Angels*, Sinclair-Stevenson, London, 1991.
——: *The Albatross and Other Stories*, Penguin Books, Harmondsworth, 1974, repr. with an Afterword 1989.
——: *The Bird of Night*, Penguin Books, Harmondsworth, 1976.
——: *A Bit of Singing and Dancing* (short stories), Penguin Books, Harmondsworth, 1976.
——: *A Change for the Better*, Uniform edition, Hamish Hamilton, London, 1976; Penguin Books, Harmondsworth, 1976.
——: *Family*, Michael Joseph, London, 1989; Penguin Books, Harmondsworth, 1990.
——: *Gentleman and Ladies*, Penguin Books, Harmondsworth, 1980.
——: *In the Springtime of the Year*, Penguin Books, Harmondsworth, 1977.
——: *Lanterns across the Snow*, Michael Joseph, London, 1987; Penguin Books, Harmondsworth, 1989.
——: *The Magic Apple Tree*, Hamish Hamilton, London, 1982; Penguin Books, Harmondsworth, 1983.
——: *The Spirit of the Cotswolds*, Michael Joseph, London, 1990.
——: *Strange Meeting*, Penguin Books, Harmondsworth, 1973; Longman Imprint Books, Harlow, 1984.
——: *Through the Kitchen Window*, Penguin Books, Harmondsworth, 1990.
——: *The Woman in Black*, Penguin Books, Harmondsworth, 1984; Longman Imprint Books, Harlow, 1989.

All these titles and editions are in print and available at present. You might find it interesting and useful to read one or two other novels by Susan Hill.

The author of these notes

HANA SAMBROOK was educated at the Charles University in Prague and at the University of Edinburgh. She worked as editor in educational publishing and was for some years on the staff of the Edinburgh University Library. Now a freelance editor in London, she is the author of York Notes on *The Tenant of Wildfell Hall*, *Lark Rise to Candleford*, *Victory*, *My Family and Other Animals*, and *Selected Works of Sylvia Plath*.

York Notes: list of titles

CHINUA ACHEBE
  Things Fall Apart
EDWARD ALBEE
  Who's Afraid of Virginia Woolf?
ANONYMOUS
  Beowulf
  Everyman
W. H. AUDEN
  Selected Poems
JANE AUSTEN
  Emma
  Mansfield Park
  Northanger Abbey
  Persuasion
  Pride and Prejudice
  Sense and Sensibility
SAMUEL BECKETT
  Waiting for Godot
ARNOLD BENNETT
  The Card
JOHN BETJEMAN
  Selected Poems
WILLIAM BLAKE
  Songs of Innocence, Songs of Experience
ROBERT BOLT
  A Man For All Seasons
HAROLD BRIGHOUSE
  Hobson's Choice
ANNE BRONTË
  The Tenant of Wildfell Hall
CHARLOTTE BRONTË
  Jane Eyre
EMILY BRONTË
  Wuthering Heights
ROBERT BROWNING
  Men and Women
JOHN BUCHAN
  The Thirty-Nine Steps
JOHN BUNYAN
  The Pilgrim's Progress
BYRON
  Selected Poems
GEOFFREY CHAUCER
  Prologue to the Canterbury Tales
  The Clerk's Tale
  The Franklin's Tale
  The Knight's Tale
  The Merchant's Tale
  The Miller's Tale
  The Nun's Priest's Tale

The Pardoner's Tale
The Wife of Bath's Tale
Troilus and Criseyde
SAMUEL TAYLOR COLERIDGE
  Selected Poems
SIR ARTHUR CONAN DOYLE
  The Hound of the Baskervilles
WILLIAM CONGREVE
  The Way of the World
JOSEPH CONRAD
  Heart of Darkness
STEPHEN CRANE
  The Red Badge of Courage
BRUCE DAWE
  Selected Poems
DANIEL DEFOE
  Moll Flanders
  Robinson Crusoe
WALTER DE LA MARE
  Selected Poems
SHELAGH DELANEY
  A Taste of Honey
CHARLES DICKENS
  A Tale of Two Cities
  Bleak House
  David Copperfield
  Great Expectations
  Hard Times
  Oliver Twist
  The Pickwick Papers
EMILY DICKINSON
  Selected Poems
JOHN DONNE
  Selected Poems
GERALD DURRELL
  My Family and Other Animals
GEORGE ELIOT
  Middlemarch
  Silas Marner
  The Mill on the Floss
T. S. ELIOT
  Four Quartets
  Murder in the Cathedral
  Selected Poems
  The Cocktail Party
  The Waste Land
J. G. FARRELL
  The Siege of Krishnapur
WILLIAM FAULKNER
  The Sound and the Fury

HENRY FIELDING
Joseph Andrews
Tom Jones

F. SCOTT FITZGERALD
Tender is the Night
The Great Gatsby

GUSTAVE FLAUBERT
Madame Bovary

E. M. FORSTER
A Passage to India
Howards End

JOHN FOWLES
The French Lieutenant's Woman

JOHN GALSWORTHY
Strife

MRS GASKELL
North and South

WILLIAM GOLDING
Lord of the Flies
The Spire

OLIVER GOLDSMITH
She Stoops to Conquer
The Vicar of Wakefield

ROBERT GRAVES
Goodbye to All That

GRAHAM GREENE
Brighton Rock
The Heart of the Matter
The Power and the Glory

WILLIS HALL
The Long and the Short and the Tall

THOMAS HARDY
Far from the Madding Crowd
Jude the Obscure
Selected Poems
Tess of the D'Urbervilles
The Mayor of Casterbridge
The Return of the Native
The Woodlanders

L. P. HARTLEY
The Go-Between

NATHANIEL HAWTHORNE
The Scarlet Letter

SEAMUS HEANEY
Selected Poems

ERNEST HEMINGWAY
A Farewell to Arms
The Old Man and the Sea

SUSAN HILL
I'm the King of the Castle

BARRY HINES
Kes

HOMER
The Iliad
The Odyssey

GERARD MANLEY HOPKINS
Selected Poems

TED HUGHES
Selected Poems

ALDOUS HUXLEY
Brave New World

HENRIK IBSEN
A Doll's House

HENRY JAMES
The Portrait of a Lady
Washington Square

BEN JONSON
The Alchemist
Volpone

JAMES JOYCE
A Portrait of the Artist as a Young Man
Dubliners

JOHN KEATS
Selected Poems

PHILIP LARKIN
Selected Poems

D. H. LAWRENCE
Selected Short Stories
Sons and Lovers
The Rainbow
Women in Love

HARPER LEE
To Kill a Mocking-Bird

LAURIE LEE
Cider with Rosie

CHRISTOPHER MARLOWE
Doctor Faustus

HERMAN MELVILLE
Moby Dick

THOMAS MIDDLETON and WILLIAM ROWLEY
The Changeling

ARTHUR MILLER
A View from the Bridge
Death of a Salesman
The Crucible

JOHN MILTON
Paradise Lost I & II
Paradise Lost IV & IX
Selected Poems

V. S. NAIPAUL
A House for Mr Biswas

ROBERT O'BRIEN
Z for Zachariah

SEAN O'CASEY
Juno and the Paycock

GEORGE ORWELL
Animal Farm
Nineteen Eighty-four

JOHN OSBORNE
Look Back in Anger
WILFRED OWEN
Selected Poems
ALAN PATON
Cry, The Beloved Country
THOMAS LOVE PEACOCK
Nightmare Abbey and *Crotchet Castle*
HAROLD PINTER
The Caretaker
SYLVIA PLATH
Selected Works
PLATO
The Republic
ALEXANDER POPE
Selected Poems
J. B. PRIESTLEY
An Inspector Calls
WILLIAM SHAKESPEARE
A Midsummer Night's Dream
Antony and Cleopatra
As You Like It
Coriolanus
Hamlet
Henry IV Part I
Henry IV Part II
Henry V
Julius Caesar
King Lear
Macbeth
Measure for Measure
Much Ado About Nothing
Othello
Richard II
Richard III
Romeo and Juliet
Sonnets
The Merchant of Venice
The Taming of the Shrew
The Tempest
The Winter's Tale
Troilus and Cressida
Twelfth Night
GEORGE BERNARD SHAW
Arms and the Man
Candida
Pygmalion
Saint Joan
The Devil's Disciple
MARY SHELLEY
Frankenstein
PERCY BYSSHE SHELLEY
Selected Poems
RICHARD BRINSLEY SHERIDAN
The Rivals

R. C. SHERRIFF
Journey's End
JOHN STEINBECK
Of Mice and Men
The Grapes of Wrath
The Pearl
LAURENCE STERNE
A Sentimental Journey
Tristram Shandy
TOM STOPPARD
Professional Foul
Rosencrantz and Guildenstern are Dead
JONATHAN SWIFT
Gulliver's Travels
JOHN MILLINGTON SYNGE
The Playboy of the Western World
TENNYSON
Selected Poems
W. M. THACKERAY
Vanity Fair
J. R. R. TOLKIEN
The Hobbit
MARK TWAIN
Huckleberry Finn
Tom Sawyer
VIRGIL
The Aeneid
ALICE WALKER
The Color Purple
KEITH WATERHOUSE
Billy Liar
EVELYN WAUGH
Decline and Fall
JOHN WEBSTER
The Duchess of Malfi
OSCAR WILDE
The Importance of Being Earnest
THORNTON WILDER
Our Town
TENNESSEE WILLIAMS
The Glass Menagerie
VIRGINIA WOOLF
Mrs Dalloway
To the Lighthouse
WILLIAM WORDSWORTH
Selected Poems
WILLIAM WYCHERLEY
The Country Wife
W. B. YEATS
Selected Poems

York Handbooks: list of titles

YORK HANDBOOKS form a companion series to York Notes and are designed to meet the wider needs of students of English and related fields. Each volume is a compact study of a given subject area, written by an authority with experience in communicating the essential ideas to students at all levels.